Teaching Subjects In Between:

Feminist Politics, Disciplines, Generations

Therese Garstenauer (coordinator)
Josefina Bueno Alonso
Silvia Caporale Bizzini
Biljana Kašić
Iris van der Tuin

RAW
NERVE
BOOKS

Series title: Travelling Concepts in Feminist Pedagogy: European Perspectives
Series editors: Clare Hemmings and Ann Kaloski-Naylor

SERIES TITLE: Travelling Concepts in Feminist Pedagogy: European Perspectives
SERIES EDITORS: Clare Hemmings and Ann Kaloski-Naylor
BOOKLET TITLE: Teaching Subjects In Between: Feminist Politics, Disciplines, Generations
AUTHORS: Therese Garstenauer (coordinator), Josefina Bueno Alonso, Silvia Caporale Bizzini, Biljana Kašić, Iris van der Tuin.
DESIGN: Hilary Kay Doran; mandela images adapted by Josephine Wilson from Ulla Holm's photographs
PRINTING: York Publishing Services Limited, UK. www.yps-publishing.co.uk
PROOFING: Karen Coulter, Lee Ronald and Liz Sourbut
FINANCIAL SUPPORT: Centre for Women's Studies, University of York, UK www.york.ac.uk/inst/cws
and Athena 2 Advanced Thematic Network in European Women's Studies www.athena2.org
WEB: www.travellingconcepts.net
EMAIL: info@travellingconcepts.net

ISBN: 0-9553586-3-9; 978-0-9553586-3-0

First published in 2006 by
Raw Nerve Books Limited
Centre for Women's Studies, University of York, York YO10 5DD, England
www.rawnervebooks.co.uk

British Library Cataloguing-in publication Data.
A catalogue record for this book is available from the British Library.

Series Preface

Travelling Concepts in Feminist Pedagogy: European Perspectives *is one of the projects currently taking place under the umbrella of Athena, which is a Socrates Thematic Network Project bringing together over 100 Women's and Gender Studies programmes, institutes and documentation centres across Europe. www.athena2.org*

The twenty-four partners working within *Travelling Concepts* have come together in the shared desire to track the movement of key feminist ideas across the geographical, political and cultural complexity that is contemporary Europe.

The partners in *Travelling Concepts* come from fourteen different European countries, and are housed within a range of disciplines or interdisciplinary contexts. Some of us work within Gender or Women's Studies departments, centres or institutes, while others negotiate the specific challenges of feminist research and pedagogy from within 'home' disciplines. Some of us work centrally within academic inquiry, while others straddle academic and activist interests, or teach within a broader educational field, such as adult education. These differing contexts invariably produce different intellectual and political agendas within the group, yet there are a number of points of commonality that we have been able to identify, and the differences have also been productive arenas of inquiry in their own right.

Intellectually and politically, thinking about travelling concepts in feminist pedagogy means foregrounding questions of exclusion, power and silence, among us and in Europe more generally. This work has to attend not only to racism and heterosexism as well as sexism, but also to the specificities of whose movements are constrained and curtailed, whose left more open. Within the work of *Travelling Concepts* West/East barriers proved difficult to overcome, as did presumptions based on generational differences, and silences around whiteness. We have been concerned to make sure that the work we produce reflects directly on these issues and is an invested, politically and intellectually charged map of conceptual travel, one in which we are all staked and located.

One of the ways we hope to develop broader dialogue is through this book series. Each of the four publications addresses a cluster of key concepts and each has been written by a different group of feminist academics from different European countries and disciplinary backgrounds. We look forward to further discussion and invite you to our participatory web site: www.travellingconcepts.net

Books

ReSisters in Conversation: Representation Responsibility Complexity Pedagogy
Giovanna Covi (coordinator), Joan Anim-Addo, Liana Borghi, Luz Gómez García, Sara Goodman, Sabine Grenz, Mina Karavanta.
ISBN: 0-9553586-0-4; 978-0-9553586-0-9

Practising Interdisciplinarity in Gender Studies
Veronica Vasterling (coordinator), Enikő Demény, Clare Hemmings, Ulla Holm, Päivi Korvajärvi, Theodossia-Soula Pavlidou,
ISBN: 0-9553586-1-2; 978-0-9553586-1-6

Common Passion, Different Voices: Reflections on Citizenship and Intersubjectivity
Eva Skærbæk (coordinator), Dasa Duhaček, Elena Pulcini, Melita Richter.
ISBN: 0-9553586-2-0; 978 0 9553586 2-3

Teaching Subjects In Between: Feminist Politics, Disciplines, Generations
Therese Garstenauer (coordinator), Josefina Bueno Alonso, Silvia Caporale Bizzini, Biljana Kašić, Iris van der Tuin.
ISBN: 0-9553586-3-9; 978-0-9553586-3-0

Details of all four books are available on www.rawnervebooks.co.uk
Books can be ordered direct from Raw Nerve or from good bookshops.

Contents

Introduction

This booklet is the result of a collaborative process between five feminist academics who live and work in various parts of Europe. We first came together in Helsinki in 2004 as one subgroup of the Teaching Travelling Concepts in European Women's Studies group within ATHENA 2. Our work is an attempt to tackle the topics 'Politics', 'Disciplines' and 'Generations' as they relate to feminist pedagogy, and we use discussion, the comparison of notes and more in-depth reflection to do so. The booklet is divided into two parts. The first section is an account of our roundtable discussion which began at a meeting in London during September 2004, an exchange of ideas which was enriched by subsequent comments and conversations both online and face-to-face. The second section positions each of the five members of the group within their respective teaching locations and relates the pedagogical praxis discussed in the first part to specific contexts.

The form that has been chosen for the booklet is a multi-layered one: the reader will find the various stages of the collaborative process reflected in the different strata of the texts and parts of the booklet. Alongside our discussion of pedagogical issues, we hope to demonstrate the efficacy, potential and challenges of our method. This booklet shows that collaborative work, such as a group session or roundtable in which chosen topics are reflected upon, can be a good way of opening up issues and laying bare tensions about some boundaries.[1]

The key topics we tackle in the booklet have emerged from our reflections on concepts such as location, positionality, institutional situation, subjectivity and the group's concerns about what inter/disciplinarity and inter/generationality signify within Women's and Gender Studies. Starting from a wide (and at times unclear) range of ideas we narrowed our focus to the core concepts of politics, disciplines and generations represented. From these we derived specific cases of differentiation, namely: national contexts, institutional settings (inside/outside universities; departments/administrative centres...), our respective inter/disciplinary locations and the generational and career stages of the participants. Although our initial positions within the *Travelling Concepts* group touched on issues of East/West, South/North, transitional/war, postcolonial/cultural hegemony[2], in the course of our discussions over two years we found ourselves prioritising other aspects relating to our teaching positions. Making explicit the position from which each of us is speaking was at first intended as a preparatory step but subsequently became a very central issue. We have become convinced that this is more than just an exercise in self-indulgence; rather we think that other teachers or students of Women's and Gender Studies can learn something from both our conversation and our further reflections and that they themselves may have gone through similar experiences.

Our discussions revealed both the complexity of the epistemological concerns that seem to be intrinsically interrelated in our feminist praxis as teachers and thinkers, and a sort of uneasiness in articulating Women's and Gender Studies substantive content as a joint venture in a changing European context, both within the academy and outside it. The result of such epistemological as well as geographical dis/location has sometimes rendered the process of comparing notes between the booklet's authors problematic. In spite of clearly having in mind that European Women's and Gender Studies does not presume to be a unified body in terms of conceptual drives or programme trends, we had not imagined the extent to which the diversity of our locations within our respective contexts and life experiences could affect the ways in which we understood (and sometimes misunderstood) each other's thoughts and dilemmas and articulated the concepts we discussed.

As mentioned above, the discussion that constitutes the basis of the first part of our booklet was taped in London and, after being transcribed, was subsequently discussed via email as well as at further meetings of the Travelling Concepts group in Thessaloniki (January 2005) and in Alicante (September 2005). During this time, several versions of the transcript travelled back and forth among us. In this process, some preliminary ideas were transformed, some new emphases were introduced and some approaches shifted from the positions taken within the initial discussion.

The papers that form the second part of the booklet (written in Alicante, Vienna, Zagreb, and Utrecht respectively – or in between, travelling…) all elaborate on positionality, institutionalisation and inter/disciplinarity. Biljana Kašić addresses the 'in-between' as both a powerful and intriguing concept for a feminist stance that has a subversive potential in epistemological mapping. Her paper explores the concept of 'in-between', using the example of Women's Studies in Zagreb as a basis for a critical invitation to analyse many related and contested concepts, processes and discursive practices around centre/ margin, activism/academism, disciplines/epistemic alliances etc. Silvia Caporale Bizzini goes into the meaning of erasing boundaries among genres and disciplines through writing and, in so doing, considers a subject that takes shape in-between discourses. She believes that the literary processes involved in her teaching practice – both when writing the text and when decoding it – are firmly based on an ontological perception of the role that writing takes up in the (de)construction of subjectivity. As Kathleen McCormick points out[3], the aim of pedagogical practice which is based on the student/reader's response to a proposed text, is to teach her to understand literary as well as cultural narrative(s) as one of the existing nodal points in the wider net of signification within power/knowledge relation. It is in this sense that Caporale believes that pedagogical practice must be able to train the student to face the literary text as a complex and historically determined net of meanings that are structured around notions of gender, race, social class and sexual orientation. Therese Garstenauer questions the seemingly universal interdisciplinarity of European Women's/Gender Studies and urges us to take a closer look at the many different agendas, conditions and approaches involved in such an assumption. Thereby, she is not calling for maintenance or re-installation of rigid disciplinary boundaries, but rather for a stock-taking of what we bring along from our training and research trajectories, instead of smoothing it all out the umbrella term 'Women's and Gender Studies'. This includes, among other things, asking the questions: (1) Are there implicit dominant disciplines in Women's and Gender Studies and (2) What is the relationship between empirical and theoretical scholarship within Women's and Gender Studies? Josefina Bueno Alonso analyses newly emerging feminism in Francophone postcolonial discourse, based on Maghrebian women's texts. Their writings reflect the difficult and even contradictory nature of the relationship between France (Europe) and Maghreb (Africa), the historical legacy and the cultural hegemony in the very heart of contemporary society. She points to a new discourse focused on both gendered and cultural dimensions. From these texts – fictional texts with autobiographical traces – we can discern a sociological discourse that facilitates a new definition of European identity and gender theory in accordance with the new millennium. Iris van der Tuin discusses generationality as one form of positioning, that is important in the context of (feminist) pedagogy. Women's and Gender Studies is now more than twenty-five years old. Rosi Braidotti has argued that feminist philosophy finds itself in a new situation: it can nowadays rely on an extensive archive of feminist scholarship. She even claims that this is but one sign of what she takes to be a fact: 'feminist philosophy has moved beyond the premises that mark its beginnings'.[4] On a more practical level we can add that the field is starting to employ a new generation of scholars. And this means that we can no longer assume that the teacher is always the oldest subject in the classroom. Besides, Women's and Gender Studies has always encouraged second-chance education and has experimented with different forms of (non-) leadership. Still, age differences and corresponding power differences exist between teachers and students, Second- and Third-Wave Feminism being merely two of the labels used in this context, and van der Tuin's paper addresses this, suggesting possible ways out of a rigid structure of intergenerational knowledge transfer.

To conclude, we want to point out that within the multiplicity of our feminist praxis and theoretical locations, pedagogy is the connecting thread. All the authors involved in the production of this booklet are teachers who have gone through phases of designing feminist educational strategies and, at the same time, are committed to feminist research. The results of our experience show that European Women's and Gender Studies scholars are in many ways (dis)connected (Domna Stanton's term)[5] and that it is of fundamental importance to problematise a universalising understanding of Women's and Gender Studies by taking a closer look at each national, institutional or disciplinary context. The multi-layering of the booklet also shows that group work is demanding and sometimes difficult as the politics of location involves the theoretical problems of 'translating' the meanings of the same concepts, notions or issues. How to agree? How to disagree? How to deal at the same time with the axes of nationality, generation, culture and the role that they play in the definition of each of our life experience? This dialogue is still open and unfinished; the importance of the dilemmas these questions open up needs continuing discussion.

Notes

[1] Please note that we write *some* boundaries. We are very well aware that the number or nature of boundaries that are paid attention to depends on how inclusive the group is. Black and lesbian feminism as well as intersectional theory are sites where this is theorised and, in fact, it is issues around 'race'/ethnicity and sexuality that are largely absent from this booklet. For a recent discussion about multiple boundaries see e.g. Feminist Challenges: Crossing Boundaries Special Issue of *Journal of International Women's Studies* 5 (3) May 2004.

[2] The position papers that represented our admission tickets to the subgroup of ATHENA 2 Teaching Travelling Concepts in European Women's Studies in the first place can be found at the subgroup's website, www.travellingconcepts.net

[3] McKormick also stresses that 'the discourse communities that dominate reading instructions and research have not adequately retheorized the reader as a social subject and the text as a social production'. See Kathleen McCormick (1996) 'Reading Lessons and Then Some: Toward Developing Dialogue between Critical Theory and Reading Theory' in James Slevin & Art Young (eds) *Critical Theory and the Teaching of Literature*, National Council of Teaching of English, Urbana, IL: 292-315, 293.

[4] Rosi Braidotti (2003) 'Feminist Philosophies' in: Mary Eagleton (ed) *A Concise Companion to Feminist Theory*, Blackwell Publishers, Oxford: 195-6.

[5] Domna C. Stanton (1985) 'Language and Revolution: The Franco-American Dis-Connection' in Hester Eisenstein & Alice Jardine (eds) *The Future of Difference*, Rutgers University Press, New Brunswick, New Jersey: 73-87.

Part One
Teaching Subjects: Facing Differences

This part of the booklet is based on the transcription of a roundtable discussion, complemented by discussions and ideas developed during the following months. It highlights what can happen when teaching subjects strike up a conversation. Teachers in European Women's and Gender Studies are divided in many respects: by national borders, institutional differences, inter/disciplinary locations, and generational differences, to mention just a few. The way we are positioned along these lines influences the way we reflect upon both our individual situation (we are teaching subjects) and more general or 'distinct' but intrinsically connected topics (such as feminist pedagogy). The politics of location is one of the epistemological foundations of the field of Women's and Gender Studies, one that is constantly under review. Do we really find ourselves confined in a certain positionality? And does such a location have strict co-ordinates?[1]

The transcription is accompanied by the voice of a narrator – composed of all our voices – that will lead the reader to those papers in the booklet's second part that connect to sections of the conversation as well as to the most important points in our group discussion. Thus the text is organised into three levels, distinguishable by their format, the statements in the first two being assignable to individual authors: (1) The main text, giving an account of the discussion, (2) the footnotes, with complementary thoughts and references to relevant literature added after the actual conversation, and (3) *the collective narrator's voice (italicised).*

The following text reflects (mostly) the chronology of our group's round-table discussion in London in September 2004. In order to make it more easily accessible, it has been edited and divided into smaller sections, each with a certain thematic focus or function. The section called **Getting Under Way** *comprises the search for a starting point. From the beginning, we find some of the participants articulating their favourite (if you will) issues. The next part named* **Who/What are the Teaching Subjects** *reflects the group's thinking about the central term, and articulates doubts about the content and adequacy of 'subjects'. In the conclusion of this section we each introduce ourselves, and describe the institutional setting in which we teach Women's and Gender Studies. In* **Contextualising I** *and* **II** *the Spanish and Croatian participants do exactly this.* **Freedom and Acknowledgement** *is a discussion that springs from the particular situation of Women's and Gender Studies in Croatia, which has the least degree of academic institutionalisation of the countries represented in the group.* **Contextualising III** *and* **IV** *sketch the conditions of Women's* *and Gender Studies in the Netherlands and Austria, respectively. The next section is called* **Resistance and Teaching** *and tackles the question of how far teaching Women's and Gender Studies can or cannot be an act of resistance. Talking about the practice of teaching leads to the next sections* **Generational Issues, Positioning oneself/Power of Naming** *and* **Inter/disciplinarity in Practice.** *The last part, called* **Activism and Bodily Issues,** *is, among other things, a reminder of things that have* not *been raised in the discussion.*

Getting Under Way

Silvia Caporale Bizzini (SCB): I realise that we all work in between, in between ideas, in between disciplines, which is our *strength* and our problem at the same time; it is a very complex approach to pedagogy and to the critical reading of society. So we can work this way: we can carry on a conversation, and then transcribe the conversation, a dialogue with multiple voices, the voice of *who* we are and *where* we stand. Each of us can work on one of the ideas we want to stress, in relation to our pedagogy, maybe to a class situation, to the necessity of teaching something, *how* to teach in relation to feminist pedagogy...

Therese Garstenauer (TG): It sounds like a very good idea, but how will we do it? We are from different disciplines; we have different ways to work, like you (*talking to Josefina*) are working on literature, mostly about these French authors...

Josefina Bueno Alonso (JBA): That is true. I am actually working with literary texts from a perspective that considers sociological discourse, which spreads from them. In the last ten years within the Francophone context in Europe new feminine voices have emerged. They have voiced their experiences through literary representation while constructing at the same time a new feminist discourse. Their writing is committed to sociological feminist issues like, for example, immigration, identity, *European* identity. It is not only a literary debate, but it becomes a sociological debate too.

SCB: I think both things are related – inter/disciplinarity and our pedagogical practices. You are focusing on an ontological discourse, but don't you think that now we can choose feminist pedagogy – more clearly, *travelling concepts* and feminist pedagogy – and we could consider the subject but also relate it to a praxis within the classroom? Maybe the most important subject in the present context is the teaching subject, and the writing subject becomes the object of the teaching subject. As in Josefina's case.

Iris van der Tuin (IvdT): The lines between the respective subjects you mention, Silvia, are not so rigid, I think.[2]

On top of pointing out our personal and pedagogic approaches we have just underlined our commitment as researchers and, most importantly, as teachers. It is precisely this commitment that has drawn us to this project contextualising our own teaching experiences in relation to Women's Studies in a European perspective. The issues of feminist pedagogy and critical readings of society will be taken up in particular by Silvia Caporale Bizzini in the second part of the booklet.

Who/What are the Teaching Subjects?

JBA: I want to stress the notion of *location*. The teaching subject is inevitably interrelated with the teaching object. My teaching experience is connected with the object of my teaching and in this sense we cannot leave aside the connection between my personal experience, my political discourse and a critical and theoretical practice in the classroom, reflected in the syllabus, that is, teaching my discipline. Francophone space – namely women's writing in a Francophone context – can be presented differently, depending on your teaching commitment. I am sceptical about the so-called intellectual 'neutrality' or 'objectivity' in our classroom.

Biljana Kašić (BK): Does this not mean that you stress our position as a teaching subject focusing on situatedness? Are we going to challenge all those issues like location, materiality, 'in between' as concerns of teaching subjects? Taking the teaching subject as a concern itself for our discussion means both to discuss and challenge the *context* and *concept* of the teaching subject.

TG: I must admit that 'subject' doesn't mean very much to me, is not the focus I usually have. I think the term subject has a substantial tradition in philosophy or psychology that I am not familiar with. Subject of course, is just a name that we can use in a way that we define. I just don't want to pretend to be somebody I am not or to know something I don't know.

SCB: But you are a subject, so you just talk about your experience. When I speak as a teaching subject in class, I usually speak of the writing subject as an object. But we don't have to forget that the writer is, at the same time, a writing subject. This means that my 'I' is narrating a situation, I talk about somebody else as an object. I am a writing subject, I can be a teaching subject, speaking subject, in the second part of this booklet I will be a writing subject, ok?

TG: Just to be precise I want to mention that we come from different disciplines. We have a common issue which should keep us together, but we could always have different associations with the same names, or even different names and associations. Mieke Bal has observed that students from different backgrounds associate different meanings with the same terms and drawing upon such experience has published the book whose title we borrowed for our group.[3]

BK: Therefore it might be good for us to contextualise ourselves a little bit in order to get more familiar with each other. I propose that each of us introduces herself to the others in terms of academic field or position.

SCB: But we are subjects in process. This conversation allows me to see some things I was not conscious of before. I've been teaching for the last fifteen years and all these things were there, some were conscious, others were not. So this conversation has clarified my ideas and what is coming out is subjectivity...

Contextualising I: Alicante, Spain

SCB: The way we are working at the university in Alicante … in Spain Women's and Gender Studies is not institutionalised in the sense that is not officially present in the university curriculum. But there are some research institutes that are carrying out the work: there are a few jobs, there are PhD programmes and things are being done. It is quite a rich landscape; we are not a research institute, we are a kind of coordination centre, but we are actually being given the freedom and the money to function more or less as a research institute, although legally we are not. It's a borderline situation, we are living in between, but we are being given funding by the university because the political will is there. Now I would like to situate our university so that you understand why we are actually surviving in between wide borders. Our university is a resilient university, a resistant university because it was the only one in Spain that at a certain point had to situate openly against the regional right wing government. So we were partially isolated for eight years. Now suddenly after the 11th of March (2004), the government changed, due to this terrible event and suddenly we, as a University, are not resistant agents any more. In spite of this, within this context our situation has not changed, so Women's and Gender Studies was resilient and is resilient; we used to be resistant agents, we still are, we are given freedom, we are tolerated, but it is like a girls' club, you know what I mean?[4]

JBA: As Silvia has said, the Centre for Women's Studies at Alicante University has a complex status. In spite of being in between institutionalisation and research and belonging to the Academy, we are still far from being recognised as an independent discipline.

SCB: I mean we are not institutionalised yet as we are not (in official terms) a research institute, but we do belong to the institution because we do get public funding from the University; it is a paradoxical situation.

We have two PhD programmes, which are politically funded because the truth is that we haven't got enough students. But, on the other side, we can't use our official teaching load to lecture in the programmes, so we teach there for free, on top of our teaching load…[5]

TG: How many of you are there, belonging to this centre?

SCB: Fifty of us, but as active members there are maybe ten of us.

IvdT: And is there a co-ordinator?

SCB: Yes, that's me. But, what if the political will in the universities is going to change? From the outside we are seen as belonging to the hegemonic group within the university, but from the inside we are not. So from the outside we belong to the hegemonic class, but from the inside we are a subaltern group. You know why borders are so important for us and the notion of being in-between discourses is also so important to us.

BK: A personal perspective is important too, or, let's say, the perspective of 'self'. It is also interesting how politics influences your position.[6]

SCB: This is why we need to institutionalise Women's and Gender Studies, because this gives you freedom, because you are within a system and the system itself is going to protect you, as long as the system works, as in the Netherlands for example. We keep on discussing this once and again, once and again in our national meetings, but why can't we do it? Because we are not able, some voices say that we are not strong enough to transform Women's and Gender Studies into a product. You sell a degree in medicine, because there are doctors, you sell a degree in civil engineering because there are engineers, but what about Women's and Gender Studies? So, this is our situation and location.

As a travelling European group, it was necessary that each of us had to introduce herself along with her institutional and national academic context. The different situations and politics of location influence our pedagogical and teaching approach. Without doubt, the politics of location as well as the politics of institutionalisation influence our position within Women's Studies, let alone the generational issue. This part of the discussion – engendered by reflection on the situation of the Spanish participants in the round table – led to a consideration of the feminist need to avoid complicity, while being aware of the fact that a certain amount of inclusion in a system that Women's Studies has set out to criticise is necessary for the survival of the institute.

Thinking of Women's and Gender Studies in terms of commodities might lead to uncomfortable feelings, even though (or rather, because) the logic of the global economy tends to occupy all areas. This type of educational engagement is not simply the use of good academic capital for the global marketing industry, but is rather a transformative potential confronting the system that provides contemporary global conditions where everything might be commodified for consumption. But at the same time how can we attract new students to enrol in these programmes if they cannot envision job opportunities or any concrete benefits out of Women's or Gender Studies in the very same market? Along with this we need new types of patrons, critical feminist ones. The papers in Part Two (especially those of Biljana Kašić, Silvia Caporale Bizzini and Josefina Buena Alonso,) suggest that an in-between-subjectivity represents (among other things) a good standpoint from which to reflect upon questions of commitment and complicity.

Contextualising II: Zagreb, Croatia

BK: Our situation in Croatia is quite the opposite, although I find some similarities. Being outside of any system we are 'free' to experiment with feminist pedagogy. Up to now, we have had no state funds we might rely on. An outsider position is our real location although some of us teach at the university as professors and guest lecturers or lead courses mostly connected with certain disciplines. Of course, we try to bring in a feminist perspective. In this regard we are almost unique in terms of creating a space for experiments in teaching or dealing with women's agendas. We are, let's say, invented subjects as both activists and feminist theorists. The students enrol in our programme not for achieving any credit (they can only get a Women's Studies certificate!), just for the pleasure of knowing; therefore it means different motivation from both sides. We have the freedom to invent our own teaching curricula due to our interest and creativity. Women's and Gender Studies is still not an academic discipline despite the fact that there are some individual efforts within already existing departments/studies and that there are some affirmative opinions among scholars towards feminist knowledge in general. We still struggle for this, becoming more and more aware that it might be easier to acknowledge 'Gender Studies' than 'Women's Studies'.

SCB: Do you think so?

Freedom and Acknowledgement

BK: Yes, I think that Gender Studies sounds much more neutral and less threatening. We can also discuss the 'neutrality' of gender and what gender means in different discourses and contexts. But what I feel now is that there are many shifting points and boundaries at the same time; so many obstacles too. I come to the point that when we address Women's Studies, we immediately face a strong type of resistance, or rather a stubborn epistemological stereotype, because within the academic field it is perceived as a political agenda. We have to be very wise to find, let's say, a sort of fluid tactic of how to interfere, of how to move forward, still preserving some utopian paths... I guess it seems to be a common point too, regardless of whether you are within the system or outside. Probably you also deal with some aspects of resistance in 'exercising' freedom.

SCB: Oh yes, I am free to teach what I want.

BK: One interesting issue which I already mentioned is about power relations and power discourse and how the donors in particular cases use power discourse for their own interests: in other words, how they try to impose their agenda through giving us funding. Our response is a type of subversive strategy. Although many of our courses are connected with the women's human rights agenda and democracy in transitional countries in a wider sense, we have no ethical problem in putting on a 'Female Hamlet', for example, or the workshop on creative writing 'Imagining the Feminine' within the same framework. In addition to this, we are getting used to, or have become very skilled and innovative in, 'translating' women's studies discourse into a meta-discourse for donors. Sometimes it is really funny, like inventing a performance, because we do perform in order to fit a certain agenda, European Union agenda, women's human rights agenda, civil society agenda, and that allows us to teach what we find crucial for Women's Studies. So this is an operation of shifting discourses; of dealing with different types of languages, administrative languages, feminist languages, neo-bureaucratic languages, and it is not easy. I think that the key problem is not to lose direction or your own meaning of existence; that is how to acknowledge the Women's Studies agenda both as an academic and as a political project.

IvdT: So in this situation you are in, Women's Studies is not recognised, but you do experience freedom?

BK: You are right. It is pure enjoyment because we have highly motivated students who come to receive knowledge and it is a different approach to studying. As I mentioned, they can only get a Women's Studies certificate, which has no meaning for our academia, but it enables them to enrol in an MA or PhD programme somewhere abroad, and some succeed.

In the last few years we have been in negotiation with the University and the Ministry of Education, Science and Sport in order to acknowledge Women's Studies or integrate it within the academic system, but it's going very slowly. So it might pass or not, it all depends on so many moments, of how the academic authority implements the Bologna process right now, or whether Women's Studies might be important in this direction. At least we can use good European examples of Women's Studies to push things forward in our context.

But what I notice now within European contexts is that some conservative trends are appearing that influence Women's Studies everywhere and it's evident that some programmes are reduced.

The Croatian situation was one of seeming paradox to many of the roundtable participants from other countries, judging by their questions. Here, there is no institutional security within the university. Ironically, the position of the Centre, which is outside the university system, seems to be secure precisely because the codes of security rely on its own assumptions, including commitment of the lecturers and possibilities to fully create and run its own programme curricula, and in that sense they experience freedom. The Croatian situation shows that the 'integration' versus 'autonomy' debate has overlooked the commonality between integration and autonomy: the fact that both imply strategies to take up within the university. The Croatian situation is one of neither integration nor autonomy in traditional terms. The Croatian situation changes the parameters of the debate, and lays bare the possibility of seeing them as two options out of, at least, three. Issues of integration versus autonomy will be reflected upon below in the discussion, and also in the papers of Biljana Kašić, Silvia Caporale Bizzini and Therese Garstenauer.

Contextualising III: Utrecht, The Netherlands

IvdT: Let me tell you the story of Utrecht, where I have worked since 2003. I must say that this story does not reflect the situation in the Netherlands as a whole. Utrecht holds a quite special position.

After the Bologna Declaration, Women's and Gender Studies has been in danger in the Netherlands. The accreditation process for Masters' degrees takes place in three steps (accreditation at faculty, university, and national levels). This means that Women's and Gender Studies can be voted down at three levels, and, indeed, reports are available of cases of voting down gender at the first two levels, which means that the third level of possible national accreditation is not even reached at many universities. Currently Utrecht is the only university in the Netherlands which offers Women's and Gender Studies programmes at all educational levels – BA, professional MA, research MA, and PhD. This means that I am both sad about the situation in the Netherlands and proud of my own programme. I will try to explain what is so special about Women's and Gender Studies in Utrecht.[7] In Utrecht our programme is well institutionalised and we have high recognition, both from students and the faculty of Arts. For instance, our courses are on several lists of optional coursework for communication students, media students, and through these lists we get a lot of students…

TG: Iris, are these courses you teach obligatory ones?

IvdT: Partly. Just to give you an example: communication studics students can choose between five methodology courses, they have five options and then one of them is Women's and Gender Studies, and this provides us with seventy-five students for our introductory course. Because of this large number of students, the programme gets money. And this is then used to offer other, more specialised, courses in which we may have fewer students, but very interested ones from all over Europe. Because in Europe we are also well-recognised, for instance through Athena.

BK: How do academic teachers from other departments/courses perceive Women's and Gender Studies at present?

IvdT: Due to the fact that our courses are sub-listed for e.g. communication studies, Women's and Gender Studies courses are recognised. And it is not for nothing that we are on the lists: at Utrecht University, students are required to do at least one methodology course, as suggested above. They can choose between several courses on quantitative research, and Women's and Gender Studies. In our faculty, Women's and Gender Studies is considered to be specialised in qualitative research. Through this whole operation we are considered specialists in the field of qualitative data processing, and have been asked to design a specific course on qualitative methodology. Of course, we have non-interested students as well, because when they come, they are looking for qualitative methods, and as soon as they understand that the object of research in all our examples has to do with Women's and Gender Studies some of the students are quite upset. Sometimes this is very frustrating for the teachers, but I think that it is good to have students learn about e.g. another objectivity, a feminist objectivity…

SCB: Don't they develop a kind of resistance in class?

IvdT: Yes, they do. Mainly the boys… They sometimes make noises, really showing symptoms of their uneasiness!

TG: I think I would find it more frustrating just to see blank faces. I find it more interesting if someone speaks up and says, 'Hey, what should this be, what is that supposed to mean?'

IvdT: Through this situation some students in the end develop the desire to do an MA in Comparative Women's Studies! They get empowered by what they learn. For instance: there is a certain resistance in the first section in the introductory (methodology) course, but as soon as their eyes have opened, or in an ideal situation, their paradigm has changed, there is the wish to know more. Of course we also have students dropping out!

Contextualising IV: Vienna, Austria

TG: Let me say a few words about the situation as it is in Vienna; this is another story. First, there is no such thing as a discipline of Women's or Gender Studies, not even a fully-fledged curriculum, so far. Women's and Gender Studies courses can be chosen as optional parts of other curricula with a modular structure. In Austria, up to now there is only one department for Women's and Gender Studies, which is at the University of Linz. In Vienna, a coordination centre is in charge of Women's and Gender Studies, and this is where I work. We provide a few introductory courses, one of which I taught last term. Most of the courses are picked from several departments. Funding for courses related to Women's or Gender Studies is provided from a special budget which was established under a female Minister of Education in the early 1980s. As for the political circumstances, I think the development in recent years of the universities in general, is more towards economy-oriented values or the university as a company. I think this has not so much to do with the current right wing government, because these things were started already when the social democrats held the majority in the government. As for Women's and Gender Studies and Feminist Studies, if we are talking about resistance, I don't see it myself as a big political actor in this regard.

Resistance and Teaching

SCB: When you talk about resistance, or a resilient subject, you don't necessarily need to have a gun to your head... I mean you just have to stand there and lecture every day, keep on working and standing up for your ideas.

TG: No, I am not talking about guns, I mean for instance, if you say that you are teaching Women's and Gender Studies for free because it is not part of your job responsibility...

SCB: I was teaching on top of my teaching load, this is what I meant!

TG: Me, I am teaching Gender Studies because I was asked to, and it is interesting *and* because I get paid for it. But I wouldn't do it for no money. Austrian universities can and do to some extent rely on the idealism of lecturers, whose affiliation to the university consists of occasional teaching and who receive little pay for that – so they are used as cheap labour.

IvdT: In my view this is a perfect example of the generational issue I raised earlier. I am also paid to teach feminism. Therese and I are from the same generation; we entered the university with Women's and Gender Studies or academic feminism already being present. We entered the university, because the university, whether it wanted it or not, needed employees that could teach Women's and Gender Studies. They had committed themselves in whatever way to Women's and Gender Studies.

SCB: You might be right, but we are not cheap[8], I don't consider myself cheap. I can teach Women's and Gender Studies in my literature course, and nobody tells me anything. I can teach Women's and Gender Studies in my PhD courses, in the English Studies Department and I am free to do it. But if I want a PhD programme in Women's and Gender Studies I have to sacrifice thirty hours of my teaching... and I do. We are talking from different contexts. When we speak of the teaching subject, we also have to speak about location, because your teaching experience is absolutely far from my teaching experience.

JBA: I think it is not only a generational issue, I think it is also a different context issue, so I agree with Silvia. In the Spanish university we belong to a recognised discipline (I work on French Studies, Literary studies) and we introduce a gender perspective into our programmes, in the classroom, but it is not a recognised discipline yet.

Many minutes are engaged in approaching a teaching position in Women's and Gender Studies including historical or cultural contexts, various disciplinary entries, models of academic settings and whether the teaching position means a commitment to women's or feminist issues first of all or rather a professional challenge; whether it comes out of activist passion or specific work in the distinctive fields of Women's or Gender Studies. But it is also an inner transformational adventure.

If we try to 'ethically negotiate' our teaching positions in this contemporary context it is more about how we connect through the system of education the necessity of affirming new knowledges with the legitimacy of verifying the material conditions of our labour. The connection between generation and academic recognition is pointed out repeatedly in this booklet. Our discussion shows how in different European locations, within or outside of academia, Women's Studies/Gender Studies have a long way to go yet – and a lot of intense discussion across borders and boundaries is needed.

Also, this debate shows how easy it is to put one's foot in one's mouth out of lack of sensitivity for the context and insult somebody without meaning to do so.

The interconnections between teaching and resistance, embedded in detailed accounts of the practice of feminist teaching will be treated in the papers of Biljana Kašić, Silvia Caporale Bizzini and Josefina Bueno Alonso in the second part of the booklet.

Generational Issues

IvdT: You know what: when I teach, I teach students that are my age. I think this is a different experience. I share a lot with my students, a cultural era, and during the break I can have conversations on culture, television… In my first year I had to buy a completely different wardrobe, because I feared that I lacked authority. I have spent hundreds of euros buying semi-professional jackets and shoes!

BK: It is amazing what we try to do in order to 'be disciplined' or acknowledged within a system.

SCB: But we all went through that phase.

TG: Well, I didn't. My students were always younger – most of them.

While this section is rather concise, the booklet as a whole does show how far generationality influences practices of European Women's/ Gender studies, and to what extent generationality intersects with inter/ disciplinarity and institutionalisation. In Iris van der Tuin's contribution to part two of the booklet, these issues will be addressed, as they will be (albeit with more focus on inter/disciplinarity) in Therese Garstenauer's.

Positioning Oneself, Power of Naming

IvdT: Let me continue trying to get across the point of the importance of the generational issue. Let me rephrase it, stressing the issue of disciplinarity/interdisciplinarity in Women's/Gender Studies: I do not teach a PhD in philosophy, nor in another discipline. I do not have a job in a disciplinary location. I have entered the university via Women's and Gender Studies, that is via an interdisciplinarity, sometimes even called trans- or post-disciplinarity.[9]

TG: Me too, but my job is an administrative one, and as such teaching is an extra job, and if I want to do research, I must do it in my spare time, provided there is any left.

BK: Your place of identification, namely the first entry into the academic world, is Women's and Gender Studies?

IvdT: Yes, I cannot speak from a disciplinary location, because I am in Women's and Gender Studies.

TG: It is also important there is something like a department of Women's and Gender Studies. There is something more I would like to add; one reason why there is no Women's and Gender Studies department at our university was the deliberate policy of Austrian Women's and Gender Studies scholars not to have departments in order to avoid ghettoisation. I am not sure whether this could be called a multidisciplinary approach, but it implies that Women's and Gender Studies should be part of every discipline there is, and not a meta-discipline in its own right.

SCB: This is the same situation as we have. On the one side, our research interest is acknowledged, on the other side there isn't a specialisation in Gender Studies. So we need to belong to a recognised discipline, English Studies (Literary Studies) in my case, to grant you academic promotions or even a job.

TG: There has been an EU-project, I think you know about it, about the institutionalisation of Women's Studies in Europe.[10] It has shown that one very crucial criterion for the successful establishment of Women's Studies is the existence of departments. I fully agree with that from a strategic point of view but I am not too sure from my personal point of view as a researcher whether it makes sense.

BK: It is of course a strategic issue connected with the problem of naming. First you have to get the power of naming, to say: 'Yes – we are Women's Studies because it is our epistemological, ethical, political whatever, point or place of identification', and then you are in the position to 'dare' or to take critical stands toward other disciplines or other epistemological fields.

Looking at it historically, contemporary well-known academic disciplines passed through the same process of acknowledgment. Even then, we can speak of a power imbalance. Right now we have parallel 'official' traditional disciplines as well as Women's Studies, Postcolonial Studies, Cultural Studies etc, those that claim trans-disciplinary, multi-disciplinary or post-disciplinary approaches.[11]

We have faced hypocrisy in the approaches to academic disciplines or fields all the time. For example, sociology in former Yugoslavia, especially during the 1940s and 1950s, was perceived as a bourgeois discipline and that its place was not at the university due to political and Marxist theoretical reasons. It took almost fifteen years to be acknowledged as a proper academic discipline. Right now, the same is happening to Women's Studies, although the resisting points are not quite as transparent.[12]

Biljana Kašić goes into the issues of positioning oneself and the power/ use of names such as Women's Studies in more detail in her paper.

Inter/disciplinarity in Practice

TG: And the next question of course is how would you teach that interdisciplinarity without being superficial?

BK: I am not quite sure what superficial means in terms of interdisciplinarity and in terms of Women's Studies as an interdisciplinary field.

TG: A little bit about everything…

BK: It is a huge landscape, the Women's Studies area, and then you enter all the other studies that mark interdisciplinarity or transdisciplinarity such as, for example, Cultural Studies. I think that the kind of discourse that is used within these studies is something else. Although the dilemma is still to what extent we can say that the points or approaches are completely new. In terms of epistemology we have to invent a lot of capacity to shift the uncertainties around.

IvdT: Actually, what do you mean by superficial? Because I consider Women's Studies and Gender Theory to be highly specialised. For instance, when I see my colleagues in another Humanities department teach, we can, from a Women's Studies perspective, always talk with them, we have things to add, we have extra layers to provide them with, to make their analyses more complex. I want to say that we are highly specialised, but we also have very sophisticated epistemological and theoretical debates through which connections with 'mainstream' disciplines are secured.

(…)

TG: I think it is useful to have a profound base in one discipline as a start, to begin looking to other fields, to other approaches, techniques and so on.

IvdT: But don't you think that you can position yourself clearly from within a Women's and Gender Studies position?[13]

TG: Still, speaking for myself, I don't think so.

IvdT: You need a disciplinary location?

TG: Women's and Gender Studies is actually just one part of what I have been trained for, but it is not my particular first interest. I would feel too limited to a certain field of research, although I find it very important to take gender aspects into account as a social scientist. So I would not position myself clearly as a Women's and Gender Studies person, although there is strong evidence that I am – considering my work place, my teaching, and also what my PhD thesis is about.

The issues of institutionalisation inter/disciplinarity and generationality kept us busy. The points of disagreement culminated here. There may, indeed, be some influence of national academic traditions here. It is not by chance that the Austrian participant insists on belonging to a discipline rather than positioning herself in an interdisciplinary field, since in German-speaking countries Women's and Gender Studies tend to be linked to disciplines more strongly than elsewhere.[14]

This creative tension on what constitutes us primarily as scholars brings to mind the constant ambiguity, or rather 'double drift', addressed by Teresa de Lauretis[15] almost twenty years ago when she tried to explore the meaning of knowledge in Feminist Studies. She spoke about the two-way process which, through producing new knowledge, not only redefines what counts as knowledge but at the same time enables the reconstituting of women as subjects of both knowledge and knowing. Relying on feminist tradition, as Iris van der Tuin suggests, at the same time means acknowledgment and 'invention' of tradition and this is not an easy task at all.

In particular, the differences within the younger generation (meaning: Iris van der Tuin and Therese Garstenauer) will be fleshed out in their contributions to the second part of the booklet. In her paper, Silvia Caporale Bizzini makes a point of breaking disciplinary boundaries within teaching practices. Josefina Bueno Alonso, for her part, focuses on a specific case of interdisciplinarity, namely the blurring of boundaries between the study of literature and sociology.

Activism and Bodily Issues

BK: All of us come through or out of disciplines, so disciplines are supposed to be a kind of secure shell, like a place we know and something we are getting used to. Personally I came out of political sciences and then I did an MA in the philosophy of art and then I embraced the theory of humanities and whatever it meant. Women's Studies issues have been this whole time my so-called 'private' interest; namely I came to Women's Studies issues primarily through my feminist activism. In the late 1980s, I became a volunteer at the first SOS hotline for abused women that was set up in Zagreb, as one of its founders. What I would like to stress is that the key point is what is one's deep location within the field of Women's Studies. From my feminist perspective the very issue of Women's Studies as well as my life itself are these locations. So it is neither discipline nor job.

Through activist work, I learned a lot about women's issues. I did research on violence against women, realising meanwhile how activism against violence against women influences the theory of violence and how the theory of violence against women influences legal sciences and so on. In short, how an activist angle at that very moment opened the door on so many levels, shifting the boundaries of disciplines and the boundaries of approaching violence at the same time and also created the theoretical paradigm of violence that happened in the late 1960s and 1970s. A very crucial issue that I became aware of later was how activism against violence fully transformed my life. So it is not a piece of patchwork or a chaotic discourse. It fulfils each aspect of my political, academic and emotional engagement. Just as right now postcolonial theory influences each entry to my activism, my writing, my approach to the world. I really feel how it interferes with and shifts the patterns of knowledge and comprehension in a very powerful manner. Feminist activism is a multilayered position which is reflected in our perception of society and theory.

SCB: It is also quite challenging because we all belong to different generations. We are located historically in different situations, in different positions.

JBA: Even our personal life, where we were born, where we live, our private experiences matter. I must say that I totally agree with Biljana. I don't know if it is due to a generational issue or whatever reason, but in my case my feminist activism is in accordance with my personal experience. I was born in France from Spanish immigrants in the 1960s and for me a Gender/Women's perspective cannot be separated from our political engagement. It is probably a different European context than Utrecht or Vienna.

IvdT: And bodily issues. Reflecting upon our conversation, I notice that we have been very good at avoiding the issue of sexuality in our conversation. Sexual difference being multi-axial, next to ethnicity and nation also sexuality is involved.

JBA: I claim our bodily issues as a starting point in our everyday commitment. We have gone through the difference of meanings of different disciplines, locations, different generations and different statuses. Now we can talk about different situations, too. As a European travelling group, we should not forget immigration as well as the perception of new coming emigrant identities.

Josefina Bueno Alonso raises the issue of immigration right at the end of the discussion, and in so doing points to an absence of issues that might have become central points in an exchange about positioning oneself in the context of European Women's/Gender Studies, such as ethnic/cultural/ religious points of view or the connection between racism and sexism. They are, however, elaborated in Josefina's paper in the following part of the booklet.

Notes

[1] Karen Barad (2001) 'Re(con)figuring Space, Time, and Matter' in Marianne DeKoven (ed) *Feminist Locations: Global and Local, Theory and Practice*, Rutgers University Press, New Brunswick, New Jersey: 75-109.

[2] IvdT: But I do think that there are certain differences that matter, when it comes to teaching. As a teaching subject of under 30 years old, I teach texts of the second feminist wave in the BA-course 'Historiography of Feminist Ideas' that runs every year at Utrecht University. These texts were written by feminists of my age – Shulamith Firestone was in her twenties when she published the *Dialectic of Sex*! (Shulamith Firestone (1972) *The Dialectic of Sex*, Paladin, London) – yet in a

completely different context. Now I teach these texts to students that are my age, or sometimes older than me, sometimes they are even positioned differently when it comes to generationality. Generational differences matter to me, especially in the context of pedagogy.

[3] Mieke Bal (2002) *Travelling Concepts in the Humanities: A Rough Guide,* Toronto University Press, Toronto.

[4] SCB: It has to be noted that since this conversation, the socialist government in Spain is carrying out an active politics focused on gender issues and seems to be willing to include Gender Studies in the official academic curricula.

[5] JBA: At the moment, Spain is carrying out the Bologna process in university studies. We have had some discussions as regards the introduction of Women's/ Gender Studies master degrees and we think that the Spanish Ministry of Education should bring Women's/Gender Studies into the official academic curricula. Without this, it will be difficult to have a recognised academic knowledge in Women's/Gender Studies, only a 'transversal' issue among different recognised disciplines.

[6] BK: From a self-referential point towards a position as such it is also, as Judith Butler points out '(…) a matter of a certain authorizing power, and that clearly does not emanate from the position itself.' Cf. Judith Butler (1995) 'Contingent foundations. Feminism and the Question of 'Postmodernism' in Seyla Benhabib, Judith Butler, Drucilla Cornell & Nancy Frazer (eds) *Feminist Contentions. A Philosophical Exchange*, Routledge, London & New York: 35-57, 42.

[7] See Jeannette van der Sanden (2003) *Truth or Dare? Fifteen Years of Women's Studies at Utrecht University 1988-2003,* Utrecht University, Women's Studies, Faculty of Arts, Utrecht

[8] This assertion can seem shocking. It is in fact partially decontextualised. I was actually answering Therese Garstenauer, who had criticised the more and more widespread habit of hiring instructors on a temporary basis and, or so I thought,

compared it to our need to teach on top of our teaching load in the programmes of Women's Studies.

[9] Nina Lykke (2004) 'Women's/Gender/Feminist Studies: a Post-disciplinary Discipline' in Rosi Braidotti, Edyta Just & Marlise Mensink (eds) *The Making of European Women's Studies Vol V*, Utrecht University, Utrecht: 91-102.

[10] TG: The project 'Women's Studies and Women's Employment in Europe' was completed in 2003. Its results have been published subsequently: Gabriele Griffin (2004) (ed) *Employment, Equal Opportunities and Women's Studies: Women's Experiences in Seven European Countrie*s, Ulrike Helmer,. Koenigstein/ Taunus, and Gabriele Griffin (2005) (ed) *Doing Women's Studies: Employment Opportunities, Personal Impacts and Social Consequences*, ZED Books, London.

[11] BK: Although the fact that two models of women's/gender studies exist in parallel – an integrational one that means incorporation of women's/gender issues or perspectives within traditional disciplines and an autonomous one in view of departments, centres or institutes, there is a dilemma about which strategic approach might correspond better to feminist epistemological claims. Feminist epistemology explores a sort of uneasy alliance of feminism and feminist subjectivity and traditional epistemology (Linda Alcoff, Elizabeth Potter, Teresa de Lauretis) including epistemic agency and the nature of knowledge itself by crossing disciplinary boundaries, expanding the spaces of disciplines and first of all shifting the focus from the discipline to the issue/subject itself.

[12] BK: Being acknowledged as Women's Studies within the Croatian academic mainstream at present is what I anticipate will happen via political will or through the framework of the Bologna Process rather than through any scholars concurrence or joint arrangement. There are two possible explanations for this: the arrogance of ignorance among scholars or a floating idea that feminism is démodé. Going towards mainstream feminism, for example, implies one's own personal commitment as well as the use of different strategies. I insist on clear and direct discursive naming as I practise right now concerning my courses

otherwise the goals or impacts of teaching can easily be neutralised. You can literally feel how the critical stands can be co-opted in favour of keeping 'order'.

[13] IvdT: In this context a quote from Linda Martín Alcoff is very important to me. She stresses that Women's Studies, in her case feminist philosophy, has been very succesful. Sometimes, she shows, the traditional relation of feminists-critiquing-the-mainstream is even reversed! 'The story of feminist philosophy has multiple plots. There is now a generation of mature thinkers, a considerable body of work, fully developed sub-areas, and even a bit of recognition. Habermas has had to respond to Nancy Fraser, Derrida to Judith Butler, and Rawls to Susan Moller Okin' (Linda Martín Alcoff (2000) 'Philosophy matters: A review of recent work in feminist philosophy' in *Signs: Journal of Women in Culture and Society* 25 (3): 841-882, 841). Here we see, again, that the issue of inter/disciplinarity is linked to the issue of inter/generationality. I interpret Alcoff's statement as follows: with the maturisation of feminist philosophy, which is but one area of Women's and Gender Studies, there is such a thing as a feminist philosophical positioning, which is, of course, not unique. No longer are we Derrideans, or Foucauldians, or Deleuzeans. We are feminist scholars working in the tradition of Haraway, or Butler, or Braidotti.

[14] See e.g. Simone Mazari, Ute Gerhard & Ulla Wischermann (2002) 'Germany' in Gabriele Griffin (ed) *Women's Employment. Women's Studies and Equal Opportunities 1945-2001. Reports from nine European Countries*, Hull University, Hull: 393-426. Another indication: One widely used German language introduction to Gender Studies is clearly structured in disciplinary chapters (Cf. Christina von Braun & Inge Stephan (2000) (eds) Gender Studien. Eine Einführung, Metzler, Stuttgart, Weimar.

[15] BK: Teresa de Lauretis (1986) 'Feminist Studies/Critical Studies: Issues, Terms, and Contexts' in *Feminist Studies/Critical Studies*, Indiana University Press, Bloomington: 1-20

Teaching Subjects in Between

Part Two
Con-Textualising the Teaching Subject

Biljana Kašić
'In Between' position

When I took on the challenge of inscribing the meaning of the concept 'in between' in terms of Women's Studies content and status as well as pedagogy, I was not thinking primarily of the textuality of time, but rather the notion of location as an appropriate and desired entry point.

Meanwhile, I considered myself caught up in 'in between' as a position *per se*, first of all because of the rupture within recent historical time in our own context, with its disturbing and wide-ranging implications for the status of Women's Studies. In addition to the war situation in ex-Yugoslav countries during the 1990s, that time blocked certain opportunities to integrate a Women's Studies programme within academic institutional settings that were sparked a decade earlier[1]. It enabled the multiplication of marginal discourses as counter-hegemonic knowledge outside of academia, and one of the most obvious effects is, following the words of John Guillory, '(...) discourse of its own being as a kind of a community' (Guillory, 1993: 35).

The position of 'in between' – especially during the first years of the Centre for Women's Studies in Zagreb that was founded in 1995 – was a sign of both the determination or only possible situatedness in terms of context(s) particularly in relation to the production of mainstreaming (academic or political) and the appeal for re/inscribing the time loss of multiple feminist knowledge.[2] Founded in a post-war setting, the Centre could not belong to the *mainstream* because of its clear resistance[3] to the official political matrix, just as the primarily silenced, neoconservative and, in some aspects, misogynist academic (*mainstream)* community was not responsive to any form of emancipatory theories, including feminist ones. The critical framework of such a Centre enabled its founders and associates to 'posit' themselves through the articulation of the dispersed pieces of their own feminist history in order to create a meaningful feminist tradition beyond the 'space-time' lag as well as to open up new spirals forward for theoretical insights and reflections.

Consequently, in that sense, the concept of 'in between', of coding a bond or potential linkage among various moments of feminist creativity in different fields by crossing the linearity of a conventional understanding of time, of its past and its present, mirrors, to a certain extent, Homi K. Bhabha's notion of 'inbetween-ness' in his introduction to *Location of Culture* (Bhabha, 1994). That is a space 'between' communicating feminist traditions, historical periods and critical methodologies and positioning to (around) feminist subjectivity.

From the very beginning, Women's Studies was a sort of autonomous and inventive laboratory in terms of its own programme agenda, regime and values as well as a model of the self-perpetuating process of legitimation that was running within numerous contexts. Bearing this in mind, I realised how this concept might become, instead of a presumed frozen line or a map of divivisions, an active position towards dominant discursive formations and divisions.

Focusing on the educational programme, that is, its content, methods and analytic framework, there are various examples of 'mediated', or rather innovative, ways of challenging the division[4] between theoretical and activist sources of knowledge. Or, to offer concrete examples: how to confront the epistemological 'body' of feminism with real women's bodily existence through 'dancing on stage', how to experience a 'public course' in feminist video art on the Flower Square in the very centre of Zagreb.

Although the survivalist politics of taking a position on the margin can be exhausting in the long run (especially in terms of purely material existence and lack of institutional acknowledgement), it offers, as bell hooks points out, '(...) the possibility of radical perspectives from which to see and create, to imagine alternatives, new worlds' (hooks, 1990: 341). In addition, an alternative 'geography' of Women's Studies is rather connected with new epistemological challenges that show how critical theory and practice are both intrinsically interrelated and shared, as well as open to collaborative and interactive education. This means expanding the meaning/content of Women's Studies through the constant creation or support of new cycles of transformative education at local, national and regional levels. Consistently advocating an open and inviting position for cooperation towards various subjects (students, artists, scholars from different universities/disciplines) has shown itself to be quite interesting, creative and powerful in the last few years.[5]

Despite this, the already existing and inevitable centre/margin dichotomy, according to our own experience, appears simultaneously either as a real issue in terms of belonging or as a dynamic oscillation of margin and centre in terms of perspective. Namely, we have felt ourselves to be at the very centre of a Women's Studies classroom, through the production of substantial work with students, including creative thinking, performances, exchange of thoughts, exhibitions, etc., and yet very distant and displaced in relation to academic authority, regardless of the fact that many of us belong to those very same academic/scholarly settings. However paradoxical it might be, the more theoretically and critically inviting in our approach to knowledge we tried to be, the more slaps of resistance we received from the academic mainstream; the more self-empowering surroundings we tried to produce, the more arrogant rebukes from the mainstream we had to face; the more innovative and creative we were, especially in crossing disciplinary fields, the more threatening we became to the institutional 'mind'.

The complexity of our position circulating within different fields (from the emotional to political or status-wise) very often demonstrates a sort of unsolvable trap. The constant see-sawing around acknowledgment and non-acknowledgment of Women's Studies as an academic discipline, the Centre's visibility and importance when it is needed for certain purposes by the academic authorities and the disappearance of the Women's Studies body when it doesn't fit into the technology of gender mainstreaming, creates a latent tension in the negotiations over integration of Women's and Gender Studies into the Croatian academic system. This becomes even more pronounced because of the potential danger that a feminist mission towards strengthening women-oriented knowledge and research could be 'translated' by the functional codes of academic policy-makers who would rather use than acknowledge Women's Studies expertise. The on-going question is whether recognition by the mainstream is a matter of justification or, even more, of the self-realisation of Women's Studies, and, if so, what types of critical senses do we need to develop in this regard?

On the one hand, our position of 'becoming minor' (Rogoff, 2000: 128) that led us to a new understanding of a strategic sense of knowledge constitutes a pulsating oppositional stance to institutional mainstream rules; on the other hand, the same position without constant reframing of its own situatedness tends to produce internal ambiguity around minor and mainstreaming stands. I have in mind not only the production of desired curricula in Women's Studies/Gender Studies that follow trends within the neoglobal market economy and which are constantly imposed by its signs and agendas, but also the 'production' of mainstream agencies within the margins that invent a jumble of messy locations within Women's and Gender Studies projects and power relations among women. Shifting the interest from rape to trafficking in women, or from 'women and power' to 'gender and development' issues, either through financial support or through NGO stakeholders, is an illustration of that which confuses/disturbs its position. Apparently there are two mutual tendencies whose direct consequence is the creation of a new type of implicit dependency on authority with completely unreachable and uncertain implications. In an epistemological sense we struggle all the more with how to keep feminist discourse lively and visible within the politics of overgenderisation, gender mainstreaming and political correctness, bearing in mind its effects on the content of educational curricula.[6] On the other hand, we are aware of how 'the invention' of new gender experts for issues such as 'trafficking of women', 'prostitution' and 'women and the microeconomy', especially in these respective regions, relies more on the functional cooperation between state actors, financial brands and new liberal international agencies (Spivak, 1999) than on any meaningful feminist politics. The reason for resisting such procedures is as much ethical as political. Therefore a claim for an 'in-betweenness', despite the disputes around its understanding[7], is not support for the logic of 'negotiation' without a critical stand concerning both Women's Studies concepts and the historical and material conditions of women's lives and status within the concrete situation, but just the opposite. Although there have been differences in the manner of critical input within the curricula and engagement of scholars in Women's Studies, the key role of Women's Studies is examining how to strengthen the use of feminist knowledge in a more contextualised, critical and sensitive manner.

Furthermore, the position of 'in between' addresses the issue of relations between subjects and places through signifying practices and contexts that situate the Centre, giving a precise sign of where the Centre is or should be within a discursive framework of authority, or women's circles or an academic framework, as well as within the mapping of ideological as well as geographical meanings, for example,

East/West (Kašić, 2004).

In the meantime, becoming anxious about how an uncritical approach towards marginality and its self-assumed oppositional commodification might play against its own source of power, we try to express our location as being more at the crossroads, open to new collaborations that cross the minor-mainstream divide, to new risks and uncertain significations. By playing host to a feminist culture of knowledge for a long period of time in the fullest sense of hospitality, that is, by supporting and being responsive to all demands and wishes when Women's Studies matter, both in the alternative and mainstream, we have realised how each act of engagement means tracing new borders and stepping out, as well as examining internal contradictions.

Do we multiply our power by consenting to assimilation and to all the rules already established by the institutional, namely, the academic mainstream (Barada, 2003), and, if so, at what cost?

How can we redefine a point of Women's Studies origin by engaging with authentic experiences alongside constraints, utopian visions and time-lag, as well as recognising one's own heritage and the conflicts that have created these experiences?

How can we argue for a proper place free of blinding layers and levels of the gender mainstreaming 'occupation' that represents power nowadays, and at the same time persevere in the process of integration of such studies within the higher education system?

What are the symbolic markers of security in Women's Studies outside or within the mainstream surroundings and discipline shelters and where are the identity sources and spaces we might rely on?

How can we offer a feminist contextual approach to research when

'(…) patriarchal practices and discourses are differentially embedded in and work through different spaces and cultural settings (Jones III et al, 1997: xxvii)'?

I find the answers to these questions more difficult to formulate now than they were ten years ago when we first started Women's Studies. Certainly many of the dilemmas today mirror, more so now than before, the complexity of interrelatedness of the feminist epistemic terrain with the status quo.

Therefore, our search for a recognisable location that comes out of Women's Studies as our almost safe and secure epistemological territory, through which critical and very often disruptive voices have emerged in order to challenge academic centrality, seems to turn in another direction nowadays. To enable transgressions within the same epistemological field demands opening up to new forms, spaces and alliances, as well as developing a new understanding of multi-faceted positions by considering constant and potentially conflicting locations, real and imaginary. In this case, significatory practices by which the concept of 'in between' circulates and functions, is being determined or mobilised – such as activism/academism, disciplines/epistemic alliances, history/time-lag, recognition/marginalisation, East/West – might provide a possibility for new creative arrangements.

Notes

[1] During the 1980s there were some very powerful feminist circles of scholars primarily around the group *Woman and Society of the Croatian Sociology Association* which initially started with an idea of possible Women's Studies programmes.

[2] This refers to various sources of knowledge that women created during the previous decade, and which were dispersed or broken up by the war (from violence against women to imagining the feminine and feminist approaches to distorted reflections in the media).

[3] The main founders of the Centre were outstanding feminist and peace activists, artists and scholars for whom the provision of an autonomous women's space for creative potential, learning and research was a personal way of 'mental' survival. During the entire time, especially at the very beginning, the Centre for Women's Studies took on the ethical responsibility of acting against war-oriented and chauvinistic behaviour against Others, which was best seen through its organisation of the first peace conference in Croatia in 1996 (see: Kašić 1997).

[4] Referring to this very contested issue, the theory/activist divide, the Centre continually provides a 'mobile' course on 'Women, Violence, Security' that encompasses women's SOS-hot lines, counselling and human rights centres. The impact of this course very often creates new constraints and divides through the effects of subjective limits and resistance to the complexity of violence and, paradoxically, through affirmative stands that might lead to an activist position for students.

[5] The Centre has become a hotbed for numerous theoretical-cultural projects whose carriers are current/former students of Women's Studies (the most recent being FemFest, a regional event that took place in Spring 2006), as well as supporting actions for manifestations such as Gay Pride in 2005 or protests against the war (2003, 2002). The Centre's associates have both participated in the production of curricula for new programmes at universities such as the first Cultural Studies programme at the University of Rijeka, or in experimental programs at the University of Zagreb such as those for human rights and democratic citizenship especially in the domain of women's studies, and also participated in the demise of such programmes.

[6] The manner in which pressure is applied for the core curricula to be conceptualised around 'Equality among Women and Men', 'Gender and Leadership, Gender in Development, Status of Gender(s) in Transitional Countries' is both obvious and aggressive.

[7] See the critical arguments around transnational feminism given, for example, by 'red critique' feminists such as Jennifer Cotter (2002).

References

Barada, Valerija et al. (2003) *Institucionalizacija ženskih studija u Hrvatskoj – akcijsko istraživanje*, Centre for Women's Studies, Zagreb.

Bhabha, Homi K. (1994) *The Location of Culture*, (Introduction), Routledge, London & New York.

Cotter, Jennifer (2002) 'Feminism Now' in *The Red Critique: Marxist Theory and Critique of the Contemporary* 3, March/April.

(online edition: http://www.redcritique.org/MarchApril02/feminismnow.htm)

Guillory, John (1993) *Cultural Capital: The Problem of Literary Canon Formation*, University of Chicago Press, Chicago.

Jones, John Paul III et al. (1997) (eds) *Thresholds in Feminist Geography: Difference, Methodology, Representation*, Rowman and Littlefield, Lanham & New York & Boulder & Oxford.

hooks, bell (1990) 'marginality as site of resistance' in Russell Ferguson et al. (eds) *Out There: Marginalisation and Contemporary Cultures*, MIT Press, Cambridge, MA: 341-343.

Kašić, Biljana (2004) 'Féminismes "Est-Ouest" dans une perspective postcoloniale' in *Nouvelles Questions Feministes: Revue internationale francophone* 23(2): 72-86.

_____(1997) (ed) *Women and the Politics of Peace: Contributions to a Culture Of Women's Resistance* Centre for Women's Studies Zagreb, Zagreb).

Nelson, Lynn Hankinson (1993) 'Epistemological Communities' in Linda Alcoff & Elizabeth Potter (eds) *Feminist Epistemologies*, Routledge, London & New York: 121-159.

Rogoff, Irit (2000) *Terra Infirma: Geography's Visual Culture*, Routledge, London & New York.

Spivak, Gayatri Chakravorty (1999) *A Critique of Postcolonial Reason – Toward a History of the Vanishing Present*, Harvard University Press, Cambridge and London.

Silvia Caporale Bizzini
Shifting Subjects, Shifting the Borders:
Writers In-Between

My interest in the concept of subjectivity – understood as a variety of perspectives subject to constant change – gradually took shape over a four-year period, eventually emerging as a doctoral thesis in 1994. Four years later, in 1998, the University decided to create – and grant some official funding to – the actual Centre for Women's Studies. We had the first meetings during the month of May 1998 and finally went into action in December 1998. Until that moment, my personal experience of feminist studies had been strongly influenced and developed within literary studies and critical theory. As a recently tenured lecturer who had had no problem in defending her teaching project and research interests in front of a not entirely convinced but pretty understanding committee, I was not fully conscious of the importance of theorising in-betweenness (although I had written extensively about it). It was during the meetings that took place between May and December 1998, when I started working with women who belonged to other disciplines, that I experienced how 'plurality (...) produces and contains not only historical subjects, practices and beliefs, but also all possibility of difference, resistance and change' (Tavor Bannet, 1993: 44). Paradoxically, or this is what I thought at the time, the same academic establishment that had seemed to accept my theoretical and critical commitment to feminist literary criticism and women's writings, reacted with some discomfort to my growing commitment to the Centre for Women's Studies and the shift to interdisciplinarity that took place in my academic curriculum and teaching projects. In Spain, departments of Women's Studies within the university system do not exist and the few research institutes are not allowed to teach in the undergraduate programmes; sociologists, artists, nurses and critics who use feminism as a point of theoretical reference work mainly within other disciplines or within special postgraduate programmes. Within and for academia, I was not a lecturer in Women's Studies, but a lecturer in English Literature. All that I did in the field of Women's Studies had to be done after fulfilling my undergraduate and graduate teaching load in the English Department. I had to learn to subsist as a lecturer, as a member of the academic community and as an individual, in a constant borderline situation. These contradictory circumstances influenced my choice of texts and authors as well as my perception of classroom work. How could I interrelate the complex reading of reality within Women's Studies with my compulsory teaching of literature? How could I articulate complexity and the crossing of boundaries within my academic context?

While addressing these concerns in the roundtable discussion of our group in London, we realised that the consciousness of inhabiting, theoretically and as individuals, different territories in-between discourses – a difference that marks our political as well as our intellectual choices within feminism – was an issue surreptitiously present throughout our dialogue. It materialised not only within the discussion on the assessment of Women's Studies as a valuable field of study and research in academic terms, but also within a clear understanding of ourselves as historical subjects. One of the questions that originated the exchange of ideas on this matter was how each of us located herself theoretically, or not, (and I infer: as a teacher) within Women's Studies in relation to other fields of studies, namely Cultural Studies. Now, I was, and I still am, convinced that breaking boundaries is essential in the everyday practice of teaching. I do agree with Biljana Kašić when she points out that: 'In terms of epistemology we have to invent a lot of capacity to shift the uncertainties around' or with Iris van der Tuin when she stresses that the theoretical complexity of Women's Studies enriches our perception of the object of study (cf their respective statements in the round table discussion in Part One of the booklet, 'Inter/disciplinarity in Practice'). The idea that motivated my intervention on this issue is that work in the classroom should focus on that innovative and revolutionary thrust of writing that does not confine itself to the limits set by recognised styles, but on the contrary, seeks its *raison d'être* in complexity and paradox. In the current climate in which globalised visual culture has become one of the most relentless vehicles through which information is compartmentalised, literature is the means I have at my disposal to draw attention to the relationship between culture and society and call into question cultural parameters that choose to deny the presence of the 'other', not only in the process of cultural representation but also in that of production. How could this become a nodal point to be developed within the classroom? My answer was that the task of foregrounding writing projects that break the barriers between discourses and lead us to an awareness of the subject existing in-between, is of the utmost importance. My point in the roundtable discussion of our group in London was that, as a teacher, I have to transform all this into a choice of texts that represent, within the limits imposed by time, credits and type of course (graduate, undergraduate), how life experiences or bodily issues are historically determined, in order to escape essentialist readings and demonstrate how 'pedagogy… engages the specificity of contexts in which people translate private concerns into public issues' (Hernández, 1997: 3).

In this sense, I believe that it is important that students approach the study and analysis of the cultural history of a given period from a perspective that enables them not only to understand which aspects form the basis of the cultural production of that era, but also to undertake the necessary questioning of that production, the limits and boundaries that may – and indeed should – be crossed, and the presence of writers as subjects of discourses that circulate in a context of literary and epistemological hybridism.

My shifting subject is, therefore, a subject who writes while shifting consciously between discourses and materiality, who recognises that her identity as a writer originates in these while, at the same time, embracing 'other' ways of feeling and understanding her own being. If – as intellectuals such as Barthes, Foucault and Kristeva have suggested – we cannot escape from the normative pressure of language, it is equally true that there are writers like the British novelist Jenny Diski, who use the great discourses of the twentieth century to emphasise how their identities materialise through a writing that is constructed around the narration of a writing self, and which hovers *in-between* reason and senselessness, the voice of the author and the impossibility of speaking out, and the representation of a world defined by its complexity, inter-textuality, and the appropriation and reinterpretation of discourses from psychoanalysis, biology and linguistics. Another example is *Waiting in the Wings: Portrait of a Queer Motherhood* by the Chicana dramatist Cherríe Moraga, the diary of her road towards maternity (Moraga, 1997). The maternal relationship is one of the first to draw children towards the outside world (and towards an awareness of themselves); it is a very special relationship of love but also one of power, since children themselves learn very quickly to separate and recognise gender roles. They learn to associate sex with sexuality, even before becoming aware of what they are and what they represent. In this context, the hybrid literary discourse of the text, along with the use of different types of sources, serve as means of redefining a subject that moves between discourses, not accepting the truth of any, but at the same time recognising the pertinence of all. Who is Moraga? The answer is multi-faceted: she is a woman, a lesbian, a Chicana, a committed intellectual and a mother. This text defines an identity that breaks the boundaries between the public and private dimensions while defending maternity as a political option that brings humanity to the struggle.

In a short essay titled 'Difficult Joys', Hélène Cixous uses her own life experience to relate her upbringing in two countries and in several languages to the experience of writing. Cixous' writer speaks and writes in 'multiple' tongues without belonging to any of them; she can live, speak and write in each of the different languages, in each of the cultures with the differences they represent, but is always shifting from one to the other, without truly belonging to any of them: 'Writing in a foreign language, playing a foreign instrument, is it possible? Of course you become familiar with it. But the most important thing is that you never become too familiar and you never come to the point when you can hear it speak to you and you think you speak it' (1990: 12). The diversity of cultures present in the different languages provides the setting for the author and her text. It is within this framework of diversity that the female writer, according to Cixous, discovers she is able to switch. This switching or shifting may come about through language, and Cixous' linguistic endeavours move in this direction, that is, towards a writing that satisfies this need and enables the other to be, to exist in multiplicity (*penser autrement*, as Foucault would say).

Primary and secondary sources:

Bannett, Eve Tavor (1993) *Postcultural Theory: Critical Theory after the Marxist Paradigm*, Macmillan, London.

Brown, Wendy (1995) *States of Injury: Power and Freedom in Late Modernity* Princeton University Press, Princeton.

Cixous, Hélène (1990) 'Difficult Joys' in Helen Wilcox, Keith McWatters, Ann Thompson, and Linda R. Williams (eds) *The Body and the Text: Hélène Cixous Reading and Teaching*, Harvester/Wheatsheaf, London: 5-30.

Hernández, Adriana (1997) *Pedagogy, Democracy and Feminism: Rethinking the Public Sphere*, State University of New York Press, Albany, NY.

Moraga, Cherríe (1997) *Waiting in the Wings: Portrait of a Queer Motherhood,* Firebrand Books, New York.

Therese Garstenauer
Afterthoughts on (Inter)Disciplinarity and Women's/Gender Studies

Within our sub-group of *Travelling Concepts*, I have often found myself in a fairly stubborn, maybe even conservative position – and have noticed this even more when reading and re-reading the transcript of our communication. I kept asking for and pointing to differences between us, particularly regarding disciplinary differences.[1]

I do not take particular pride in this, but I simply could not help it. Whenever our group met, there was comparatively little time for our discussions. But so many things had to be explained in order to know what we were talking about. It was absolutely necessary to explain what it means, what it is like to teach Women's or Gender Studies in a certain (national, cultural) context. The transcript shows that it took us some time and talking to get to this point.

Words can be of questionable reliability. We are all teaching Women's or Gender Studies, we are all feminists, aren't we, so what? Just the short introductions presented in the conversation above make it clear that teaching Women's Studies can imply very different actions, goals, frameworks, influences and opportunities. It became especially clear with Iris van der Tuin and I who, being younger than most of the other *Travelling Concepts* members, first got in touch with Women's and Gender Studies at a point when it was already there, when there were already paid jobs – we entered the university via Women's Studies, as Iris put it (again, with a difference: her point of entry was a PhD post that includes teaching, mine was an administrative post in the Centre for Gender Studies of the University of Vienna with additional teaching courses.) Thus, for us, however passionate we might feel about Women's and Gender Studies, it is a job, and not something that must still be fought for, or constantly defended – for the time being, at least.[2]

Maybe it is due to my own academic experience that I am so wary and picky about disciplines. I studied Sociology and Russian language and literature for my diploma, and as an example, when presenting the results of my diploma thesis on Gender Studies in Russia (a sociological work with relevance to Russia), I experienced systematic misunderstanding from sociologists and Slavists alike. The problem was not their respective lack of interest in or even knowledge of Women's and Gender Studies, but different uses, different perspectives and sometimes different understandings of the same words.

My experience is that interdisciplinarity and travelling between disciplines is, plainly speaking, hard work. Lots of explanations and translations have to be made in order to understand others and to be understood correctly. Shortcuts are possible, but I do not think they do Women's and Gender Studies (or any other interdisciplinary project) any good. Answering my caveat in the London roundtable discussion of our group that interdisciplinary practice in a bad sense can turn out to be superficial, Biljana Kašić protested vividly, and Iris stated that in her opinion, Women's Studies (understood as interdisciplinary) is highly specialised. This I can and will not deny. Only, I insist that interdisciplinarity in a good sense requires great effort.[3]

I am very intrigued by the question of whether there are leading disciplines in Women's/Gender Studies, a context meant to be and declared as interdisciplinary. Leading, here, implies that they provide theory (or even Theory) that proves relevant for most if not all scholarship in Women's and Gender Studies. Judging by the backgrounds of today's stars or key theorists, such disciplines appear to be philosophy, literary theory, sociology or history. Maybe I am utterly wrong, here; surely this would call for a thorough investigation, informed by the sociology of science.[4] I have, however, made the following observation: In 2005 I organised an international conference, dealing with the question of whether or not there is a canon in Women's and Gender Studies.[5] The call for papers was addressed to scholars of Women's/Gender Studies without expressing a particular disciplinary leaning. The Call for Papers was distributed via national and international (mainly European) Women's-and-Gender-Studies-related mailing lists such as Network East-West-Women or FEMALE, a German-language mailing list for Historical and Social Sciences (HSozKult). Furthermore it was sent to European Women's and Gender Studies Centres as well as to individual scholars with whom the Centre for Gender Studies at the University of Vienna had been in contact. Due to my own research interests and the focus of the conference, this included in particular many scholars from Russia and Central Eastern Europe. It turned out that most of the proposals that were submitted came from people who work in departments of (mostly English or American) language and literature. Sociology came second. Literary scholars and sociologists taken together amounted to about half of all the proposals. I have tried to make sense of this, have thought of possible explanations. One idea was that, particularly in non-English-speaking countries, scholars of English might be more likely to get in touch with Gender Studies writings, still predominantly written in English. But then, these writings would have to have some relevance for literary scholars, either because they deal with literature, or because they are abstract (theoretical) to a point that makes them relevant to Gender scholars in all fields. Here, again, a more thorough and far-reaching investigation would be required in order to be able to present more than just hunches.

The question of disciplines also comes up when teaching, say, introductory courses in Women's and Gender Studies. You have to decide what you will include in the agenda (unless this has already been decided by others, as in Iris van der Tuin's experience in Utrecht). What do students, new to Women's/Gender Studies, need to know? I have tried to cover as much as possible, but even with a historian as co-teacher we had to leave out some subjects, discussions or methods. And so we concentrated on what we knew most about. What it boiled down to was an introduction to Gender Studies with an emphasis on historical and social science discussions.

The question of disciplines is, obviously, strongly linked with academia. Women's and Gender Studies (and even more so Feminist Studies) finds itself in a sort of schizophrenic situation, trying to gain acknowledgement within a broader scholarly community on the one hand and to criticise or even change the academic context on the other. This contradiction has been at stake ever since feminist scholars first succeeded in gaining ground within universities, and a great deal of ink has been used by more seasoned and eloquent persons than me to discuss it. Judith Stacey (2000), for one, has called academic feminism an oxymoron, i.e. a conjunction of incongruous or contradictory terms. No wonder the trade-off between academic recognition and autonomy came up as an issue in our group's discussion as well, with different emphases depending on the speaker's background. The further one is from academic institutionalisation and acknowledgement, the less one has to worry about disciplinary boundaries.

I found it noteworthy that the trade-off discussed was not only between feminist ideas and academic customs, but also involved other aspects. A dependence on the overall political situation is significant to varying degrees, as Silvia Caporale Bizzini explained, all the more so when the Women's/Gender Studies institution in question does not have a strong standing within the university. A stronger degree of institutionalisation would lead to more independence from the actual political situation, but then again requires a higher degree of adjustment to academic rules of the game. This can even concern the clothes we choose to wear when teaching – see Iris van der Tuin's story about the semi-professional jackets chosen to distinguish her from her students, who were not (much) younger than her.

Economics and the labour market also interfere: Women's/Gender Studies is seen as a product that needs a demand in order to justify its supply. The commodification of knowledge and education, the re-structuring of universities upon the model of companies, affects other fields as well. But, to take an example from the University of Vienna, which I am familiar with, if a new MA degree course in Gender Studies were developed, it would be crucial to point to its very concrete usefulness and the employability of its graduates.

Coming back to my initial argument, conservative or not, I think it is worthwhile to take differences within Women's/Gender Studies into account. By differences, I mean not just social, ethnic and other criteria that an old-fashioned sociology of science would call external. Rather, I am speaking of disciplines, approaches and even objects of one's research.[6] Thus, one could see more clearly what Women's/Gender Studies consists of and what scholars in this field actually do. Power hierarchies, inherent in academia, could be made explicit. (Is a case study of higher value than a survey? Is literary theory more important than anthropological fieldwork? Would you rather have your piece published in a US-American peer-reviewed journal or in a Russian conference volume?) Remembering Pierre Bourdieu, one could ask for the symbolic capital of Women's/Gender Studies. My point is not at all to demand the maintenance or re-installation of rigid disciplinary boundaries, but rather a stock-taking and showing of what we have at hand, what we bring along from our training and research trajectory/ies, instead of smoothing it all out under the outwardly interdisciplinary, yet strangely uniform, umbrella term Women's and Gender Studies.

Notes:

[1] I have company, it seems, since I read in Clare Hemmings' 'Telling Feminist Stories': 'In a sense then the pragmatic call for a "return" to academic common sense is also a call for disciplinary specificity, training and rigour, a challenge to the interdisciplinary eclecticism associated with poststructuralist, and of course feminist, approaches' (130). This statement refers to feminist scholars who are sceptical of progress stories about the history of feminist theory.

[2] Inferring from the configuration of our discussion group I cannot draw far-reaching conclusions about the generational settings within European Women's and Gender Studies. Also, I do not want to stage a simplifying story that goes like this: The feminists of the generation(s) before ours were activists who fought for the implementation of Women's and Gender Studies which, as a result, has been around and is here to stay. Enter the young scholars of Women's and Gender Studies who find university jobs by which they gain access to the field… One has to keep in mind that the degrees and types of institutionalisation of Women's and Gender Studies in Europe vary greatly (and, besides, that university posts are scarce). For the occupational statistics of Women's Studies graduates see Gabriele Griffin 2004, 2005.

[3] The booklet 'Practising Interdisciplinarity in Gender Studies' by Vasterling et al (2006), also developed within the *Travelling Concepts* group, takes on these very aspects in more detail.

[4] I would love to conduct such an investigation.

[5] The proceedings are forthcoming, to be published in 2006 by the Centre for Gender Studies at the University of Vienna.

[6] Taking up Sylvia Walby's (2000) argument, I would like to have taken into account both the social location and the argument.

References:

Demény, Enikö, Clare Hemmings, Ulla Holm, Päivi Korvajärvi, Theodossia-Soula Pavlidou and Veronica Vasterling (2006) *Practising Interdisciplinarity in Gender Studies* Raw Nerve, York.

Griffin, Gabriele (2004) (ed) *Employment, Equal Opportunities and Women's Studies: Women's Experiences in Seven European Countries* Ulrike Helmer, Koenigstein/Taunus.

_____ (2005) *Doing Women's Studies: Employment Opportunities, Personal Impacts and Social Consequences* ZED Books, London.

Hemmings, Clare (2005) *'Telling Feminist Stories'* in Feminist Theory 6(2): 115-139.

Stacey, Judith (2000) 'Is Academic Feminism an Oxymoron?' in *Signs* 25(4): 1189–1194.

Walby, Sylvia (2000) 'Beyond the Politics of Location: The Power of Argument in a Global Era' in *Feminist Theory* 1(2): 189-206.

Josefina Bueno Alonso
Maghrebi Women's Texts –
New Gendered Identity in Europe

My research career is related to a personal experience marked by emigration – my parents were Spanish, but I was born in France in the 1960s, where I did my primary and secondary studies – and also by having grown up and having been educated in spaces that are difficult to demarcate and that are marked by that *in between* as regards language, culture and a subjective view of what is considered to be 'national borders'. In this respect, my personal experience comes close to what Rosi Braidotti names 'nomadic consciousness' (Braidotti, 1994: 2) and I will not deny that it is also reflected in my field of research. Moreover, I felt somewhat out of place in the subgroup, fundamentally due to the fact that I do not come from the Anglo-American tradition, but from a French-Spanish one, which is far away from the dominant language and from Anglo-American feminist theory.

As regards my *Teaching Object* – literary texts – my attention is focused on a corpus that is difficult to delimit and what is more important, a corpus that finds it difficult to gain academic recognition. The so-called *Francophone Literature of the Maghreb* dates back to the 1950s and has come into being as a result of the struggles for independence of the colonies, but written in the language of the coloniser. This situation turns the texts of this period into texts with an inherent *in-between* position from creativity and fiction, but at the same time they are torn between the centre and the margins from an academic and institutional point of view.[1] Another fact that should be borne in mind is that it has to do with writers who initially came from the Maghreb, but who nowadays live in Europe and who recreate an ethnic and sociological scope that affects many European countries with a growing Maghrebi population, mainly France and more recently Spain. What I want to reflect with this brief introduction is that teaching, revealing and dealing with these texts gives rise to a doubly complex task, not only from the discipline itself, but also from its identity approach. To all of this, I should also add a gendered perspective, which would lead me to wonder what is the centre, if any, of Women's and Gender Studies theory. Or if the centre is the same for all disciplines ... (cf. also Therese Garstenauer's paper in this section).

The impact of Francophone postcolonial discourse has been felt even beyond the metropolis itself.[2] In the particular case of women, they worked closely with their male colleagues in the decolonisation process with all the complexity that being 'daughters of the colonisation' entailed, and with all the controversy that went with this name; if France is regarded as the colonising country, it can equally be regarded – either literally or figuratively – as a liberator. France and the French language have meant access to school, university, etc. Clearly then, despite the fact that French colonisation brought with it large degrees of emancipation, we hear more and more voices announcing that the delimitation of identity works interactively with other strata (Braidotti, Butler, etc.).[3] Among the aspects that Braidotti regards as being particularly significant in the case of Maghrebi women writers, are the rejection of a non-unitary conception of the female subject, the analysis of female subjectivity using a set of stratified variants (race, ethnic group, social class, etc.), and the concept of *location*. These 'emerging' voices in Francophone postcolonial literary production are in line with a 'feminist nomadic consciousness', and, in my view, constitute the main challenge currently faced by feminist thought.[4]

Discourse on women in the Maghrebi context has been particularly fruitful in the sociological sphere – especially in the field of immigration. Worthy of mention here are the classic works by Camille Lacoste-Dujardin, the studies on Maghrebi immigration carried out by the sociologist Juliette Minces, and a number of essays that denounce the repression suffered by many young women in the *banlieues* of major French cities, such as the one written by Fadela Amara which had a strong impact in the media.[5] Likewise, the work of the Moroccan sociologist Fatema Mernissi – standard reading in the West as regards the debate surrounding feminism and the Muslim woman – could equally be cited, as indeed could the work of the Turkish sociologist Nilufer Gole.[6]

In the analysis of the contribution made by women writers of Maghrebi extraction to gendered discourse, these women's experiences reflect the difficult and even contradictory nature of the relationship between France (Europe) and the Maghreb (Africa), the historical legacy and the cultural hegemony, at the very heart of contemporary society. A significant factor that should be taken into account is how fiction reveals the violence suffered by these women: the experience of the war for independence, the increase of Islamist movements in Algeria or the repression, as well as discrimination against women, are, among others, possible forms of violence and they show the resistance that is involved in women's culture. These texts also reveal the unfolding of the historical process, the ways in which these women relate to the language of the coloniser and to their culture of origin, while at the same time manifesting a European perspective, Europe being their place of origin. The work of these women displays a marked gendered perspective and a double belonging, their fiction possessing a strong autobiographical flavour, taking the form of prose and essays. The themes and motifs most frequent in their writings are their relationship with the language of writing, reflection on identity and the difficult combination of integration and assimilation.

It is necessary to point out that gendered discourse inferred from them acquires different generational nuances. If the first years represent assimilation within a universal feminism, as time goes by – in the third or fourth generation – the discourse moves gradually away from feminine universalism and we witness a more critical attitude. The most recent generation – which coincides with the works that appear at the end of the 1990s – puts forward the challenge of gendered discourse in the framework of the social tension/generation that arises from the immigrant population living in Europe. Therefore, which is the gendered discourse or the women's discourse in convergence with a different ethnic group/culture? Undoubtedly, this is an important discussion brought about in Europe and it should be taken into consideration in the field of Women's Studies.[7]

From the 1980s, this production increases extensively – coinciding with the boom of women's movements in the Maghrebi context – and becomes a place of resistance, a form of struggle against the traditional discourse transmitted by a misogynous culture supported by religious discourse.[8] In spite of it being fiction, it reveals both personal and social concerns and conflicts. While these texts echo the great figures of French feminism (Beauvoir, Cixous, Kristeva), their discourse differs considerably from feminist discourse originating within the French context. Interestingly, the first writers (e.g. Assia Djebar) to some extent assert a 'universal feminine identity' through feminine poetics, one of the most significant differences compared to Anglophone feminist theory. The fact that the first generation defends a *sisterhood* for women is due to the humanistic distinctness of French culture. For as Naomi Schor contends, French universalism refers to the achievements of the Revolution and to the Age of Enlightenment, whereas in the Anglophone tradition, this universalism would appear to be more closely linked to phallocentrism.[9]

We should also be aware of the influence that *French Feminism* had on these pioneering writers. The writings of Luce Irigaray, Hélène Cixous and Julia Kristeva have emphasised – through psychoanalytic criticism – the specificity of feminine identity as a counterpoint to the phallocentric postulates of Freudian theory. Luce Irigaray recreated a kind of idealisation of the feminine and the relationship between women. This sisterhood of women is particularly present in her description of the *hammam*. However, it is important to be aware of the risk of a possible feminine essentialism that might reinforce certain topics, which are maintained in the name of women in general and/or women from the Maghreb.

The work of these Maghrebi writers has evolved in recent years, coinciding with a foray into a new genre: the sociological essay. These writers have entered the sociological field, committed to the defence of aspects that concern women in a Western context. The fiction converges with sociological discourse, creating a new gendered discourse, the product of current confrontations in Europe, with its social imbalances and ideological tensions. First and foremost, the work of these women is marked by an ideological shift; they call into question the supposed homogeneity mentioned above that does not take into account specific differences, especially those of a socio-cultural or ethnic nature. Likewise, post-modern thought has emphasised Otherness, the Other being seen not only from a gendered perspective; a view reinforced by the flow of immigrants, the situation of neo-colonialism experienced by the immigrant population in the West, reinforcing the desire to express a specificity that is more and more distant from its 'white', Eurocentric starting point. One of the examples that illustrate this point is given by the Algerian writer Malika Mokeddem, whose 'disorientated' writing represents the nomadic consciousness that Braidotti refers to, in that it crosses borders and represents a new conception of the traditional, stereotyped dichotomy of women's versus men's writing.[10] Although sexual belonging is still very present, it does not prevail in a discourse that seeks nothing more than to reconstruct arbitrary, centralising and prescriptive categories.

These writers, despite appearing to have inherited a French culture, have never stopped belonging to a different culture, and in some cases a different religion and it is from that perspective – with all its contradictions – that they stand as a dissident collective voice that has challenged and redefined hegemonic European identity in the way attested to by Braidotti.[11] Feminist theory is faced with a social discourse present in France and in other European countries with large Maghrebi populations that frequently defend an identity different from the Western model, marked by a different religion and the result of difficulties of integration. We therefore have a gendered discourse subject to internal and external tensions that make it more and more difficult to define a female identity, to be a woman and define oneself as such. These social protests have become stigmatised and reduced to the controversial issue of the veil, which has, by metonymy, come to denote the figure of the foreigner living in the West. An example of this is the essay by the Tunisian writer Fawzia Zouari.[12] Although the veil has become a contradictory symbol with diverse connotations, one point needs to be made clear: the defence of the veil is an issue that has gone beyond strictly religious boundaries, and has become the defence of an identity. Zouari deals with the issue of the veil in France in a very direct manner. Beginning with the prologue, she states her position through negation: she claims to be neither an historian, nor a legal expert, nor an expert on Islam, but declares her intention to tackle the subject via a 'third way' with the aim of avoiding confrontation. In this book, Zouari traces the history of the use of the veil in France, and examines the various standpoints by presenting the arguments of politicians, intellectuals and social movements. The work is therefore noteworthy not only for its gender perspective, but also as a critical expression of the limits and determining factors of a European, French identity in a constant state of metamorphosis. Examples like these give an account of the historical evolution of a discourse which, starting with the defence of identity, enables the authors to elucidate current issues and challenges. This discourse is not without its tensions and conflicts, of both a personal and social nature; it reflects on European political systems, the factors that determine immigration, and the role of writing in intellectual and vital construction. The voices of these women remain an important referent in the construction of a new gendered discourse immersed in and originating from European society.

If the first generation of these writers constitutes above all a vital experience that condemns the status of women in the context of the Maghreb, it is only during the following generations that the literary discourse complements the sociological discourse and is related to a 'gendered discourse' that is closer to and more immersed in a multicultural European coexistence. Although both postcolonial and feminist theories have mainly been under Anglo-American control, we cannot forget that a different cultural origin, a different theoretical tradition, turns these voices into referents in southern Europe, characterised by the constant evolution of feminist thought. These women's experiences, marked by that 'inbetween-ness', show the challenges that Women's and Gender Studies faces and complete some creative new alliances among the geographical and epistemological limits, as Biljana Kašić emphasises in her paper, above. From her words, one of the challenge for academics in Women's/Gender Studies is perhaps to delimitate 'a safe and secure epistemological territory' where spaces and multi-faceted positions can be developed.

Notes

[1] It is important to remember that the centralism inherent to French culture and tradition, which is different from the English and Spanish-speaking contexts, means that these texts are preferably studied within the fields of comparative literature or so-called 'immigrant literature'.

[2] See Frantz Fanon's, Albert Memmi's or Tahar Ben Jelloun's works.

[3] For a general overview of female postcolonial literature, see Inmaculada Díaz-Narbona & Asunción Varó, A. (2005) (eds) *Otras mujeres, otras literaturas*, Zanzíbar, Madrid.

[4] Clearly, feminist discourse in the Muslim context does not only originate in the West, and debates on Islamic feminism are gaining in importance

[5] Camille Lacoste-Dujardin (1985) *Des mères contre les femmes. Maternité et patriarcat au Maghreb*, La Découverte, Paris; Juliette Minces (1986) La génération suivante, Flammarion, Paris; Fadela Amara (2003) Ni putes ni soumises, La Découverte, Paris.

[6] Fatema Mernissi (1991) *Marruecos a través de sus mujeres*, Ediciones del Oriente y del Mediterráneo, Madrid; Idem (2003) *El harén en Occidente*, Madrid; Nilufer Gole (2003) *Musulmanes et modernes*, La Découverte, Paris.

[7] We should point out that issue 25 of the journal *Nouvelles Questions Feministes* (2006) is devoted to the overlap between sexism and racism. It also analyses the controversy and the exploitation of the discourse about

women's rights centred on the Act banning the use of the veil in France.

[8] This approach to these writers allows us to deal with women's relations to monotheistic religions – deeply rooted in Mediterranean culture – and not only to Muslim religion. As Antoinette Fouque states: 'women suffer a structural *apartheid* inside monotheisms' (Antoinette Fouque (2004) *Il y a deux sexes*, Gallimard, Paris: 185).

[9] See Naomi Schor (1995) 'French Feminism is a Universalism' in *Differences: A Journal of Feminist Cultural Studies*, 7(1): 15-47, 21. 'What is certain is that whereas in American feminist theory there has been a tendency to extrapolate from the falseness of phallocentric universalism the notion that all universals are false, in French feminist theory the universal remains, despite all its misappropriations, a valorized category to be rethought and refashioned'.

[10] See Malika Mokeddem (2003) *La transe des insoumis*, Grasset, Paris.

[11] 'European identity has managed historically to perfect the trick that consists in passing itself off as the norm, the desirable centre, confirming all "others" to the position of periphery' (Rosi Braidotti (1994) *Nomadic Subjects: Embodiment and Sexual Difference in Contemporary Feminist Theory*, Columbia University Press, New York: 10).

[12] Fawzia Zouari (2004) *Ce voile qui déchire la France*, Ramsay, Paris.

Iris van der Tuin
The Generation Game

I have been teaching feminism and feminist theory to students who are my age for almost three years now. I started in September 2003 as a junior teacher in Women's Studies in the Faculty of Arts at Utrecht University. As a recent Women's Studies Masters graduate, I was appointed to teach in and co-ordinate three modules: the introduction to Women's Studies (BA level), a module on feminist classics (BA and MA level), and a feminist theory module (MA level). I had also completed an MA in the Philosophy of Science.

My job has been an exciting journey from the start. The students on my courses are my age, so they are my peers as well as my students. We share a cultural background; however, the audience is quite international. Moreover, I have been team-teaching with Women's/Gender Studies professors from the beginning. This gave the courses a 'generational' twist. The question 'who selects the material?' was pertinent while reflecting on the course outline, and also, 'who teaches what?' I did not write the courses that I was appointed teach – they had been set up some ten years ago, and a number of teachers had already been changing and adding to them.

My contribution focuses on generationality as being important amongst the categories that make up one's situatedness. As I stated in the round table that is reproduced in Part One of the booklet, I strongly believe in generationality, along with age, as amongst the important axes of social and cultural signification, and, consequently, of feminist reflection. I take it that one's generational position is produced in, for instance, the classroom, taking into account the fact that a classroom usually has two (often age-related) positionings present (teacher(s) and students). I also note Haraway's observation that with the coming into existence of Women's Studies, or feminist academic spaces, feminist consciousness-raising was transposed from the living rooms of second-wavers to the classroom.[1] This standpoint resonates with my own experiences as a teacher, as voiced in the round table, as well as with being a Women's Studies PhD student working with second-wave teachers and reflecting upon 'feminist (academic) classics'.

In this contribution I want to defend the following case: *a generational take on feminist theory and its developments allows for transversal lineages and genealogies that undercut a narrative structure of progress.* This is not the case solely for the generational take. Feminist theorists have been theorising advantageous and disadvantageous perspectives from the 1970s onwards. Donna Haraway is, of course, exemplary. In 'Situated Knowledges: *The Science Question in Feminism* and the Privilege of Partial Perspective' (1988)[2] she reflects on Sandra Harding's 1986 classification of feminist epistemological schools in *The Science*

Question in Feminism.[3] Haraway argues that a classificatory approach is rigid, and tends to become a narrative in which approaches solve each other's problems and become gradually better and better. Feminist scholarly practice is both more open and more complex than such a succession might suggest. Haraway's example of the feminist scholar clinging to both ends of the same stick has become famous. Complexities such as these stem from all kinds of positionalities – and I argue that generationality is one such position. I further want to argue that the generational take allows for transversal connections wherein teleologies are criticised and, in fact, through this strategy, progress narratives might even become useless: being self-reflective about one's generational position might allow for teleological reasonings to be undercut instead of easily affirmed. In other words, it is not something *inherent to* generationality to be able to recognise and discard teleological tendencies – isn't the Oedipal plot directing us towards considering ourselves as being better than our mothers? Yet because of this we might be forced into a position where we no longer see 'mothers' as our rivals. In addition, up to now most critiques of this teleological story of feminist theory have arisen in the work of black and lesbian feminists, who have argued that the way feminist theorists tell their stories has pointed to false progress.[4]

Let me illustrate my point with an example that comes from interviews I have conducted with Swedish PhD students in Gender Studies for my dissertation.[5] In these interviews 'Butler' comes to the fore as what I would label a 'generational marker.' In the context of the Swedish 1990s, students would encounter Judith Butler and queer theory more easily, and, actually, simply *earlier* in their academic career than (Swedish) feminist authors from the 1970s, 1980s, and/or 1990s. During their studies – the PhD students I interviewed usually had taken a more or less disciplinary education – the students would encounter feminist material through an addition to the syllabus (a generally gender-blind syllabus contains one gender-sensitive article or chapter) or through a feminist teacher pointing them to the matter. Usually this text or suggested reading would be work from the U.S. philosopher Judith Butler. Her *Gender Trouble: Feminism and the Subversion of Identity*, published in 1990 and reprinted with a new preface in 1999,[6] seems to have travelled the Atlantic and bedded down firmly in Sweden. (From my teaching experience, I can conclude that this Swedish case does not stand on its own.) My interviewees would narrate their journey to feminist theory and the field of Women's Studies through their encounter with Butler. Donna Haraway and occasional Swedish authors were also present in the narratives, yet much less as a 'knot' than in the case of Butler.

What does Butler as a generational marker mean? It is common to hear/tell the story of an essentialist yet activist 1970s, a 1980s that covers the black and lesbian critiques as well as the move to the university, and a 'theoretical' 1990s.[7] The theoretical 1990s, then, is presented as a feminist apotheosis: this is where it has led to, finally 'woman' got deconstructed! Through that narrative of having read Butler 'first,' the PhD students I interviewed were able to bypass common stories of the three phases of equality-difference-deconstruction. In my interviews I asked them about the theoretical framework they had set up for their dissertation. Some of them said they had gone 'back to Butler' after a period of having questioned the usefulness of her performance theories for their dissertations. While most narratives on feminist theory in fact move *towards* Butler as a feminist apotheosis, the three-stage model mentioned earlier being an exemplary case, the current generation of feminist scholars in the field of Women's or Gender Studies does away with such common teleologies. Having become interested in feminism through *Gender Trouble* and queer theory means that they have become interested in feminism through its critiques. Going 'back to the 70s', my interviewees became interested in feminism itself, and having read the original 1970s sources, they might or might not go back to Butler as 'original.'

In my example I have tried to show how theoretical trajectories of the current generation of PhD students do away with a story of progression from the 1970s to the 1990s – stories that are precisely criticised as damaging for the field of feminist theory by scholars such as Clare Hemmings. It shows that a certain authoritative, much-rehearsed reading of feminism's past is as generational as the student perspective itself. In some instances Butler or constructivist approaches are *not* what we are reading, or even where we are at.

Becoming 'third wave'

Taking a perspective to be 'generational' is not exhaustive. I have briefly commented upon the transatlantic journey that Butler's work has apparently made. In the context of feminist narratives, the transatlantic axis can be inserted by reading Hemmings and Rosi Braidotti through one another. In 'Telling Feminist Stories,' Hemmings criticises the previously mentioned common narrative for, among other things, overlooking the contribution of black feminists in the 1970s (and 1980s and 1990s) when poststructuralism gets to carry the burden of having 'finally' deconstructed 'woman.'[8] In 'The Way We Were,' Braidotti works from a European angle. She shows that in the French context it *does* make sense to say that poststructuralists engendered 'the decline of equality or emancipation feminism'. In other words: it does make sense to have poststructuralists carry the burden of a deconstruction of 'woman.' As such it is less a transatlantic disconnection that we should be researching than an Anglo-American one.[9] Braidotti shows that during the late 1970s and early 1980s French poststructuralist feminist thought *did* discard 1949 emancipation feminism (Simone de Beauvoir), thus providing us with an example of how an insertion of sexual difference or 'French feminism' gives an entirely different genealogy. Reading Hemmings with Braidotti, it becomes clear that both the dominant narrative *and* the deconstructive narrative are part of the dominant Anglo-American story.

A concept that has become inextricably connected with thinking about the generational in a contemporary feminist context is the 'third wave.' With *feminist.com* being a 1995 New York initiative and Astrid Henry's *Not My Mother's Sister: Third Wave Feminism and Generational Conflict*[10] crowded with North-American texts, we should not be surprised to find younger *European* feminists hesitant when it comes to naming themselves 'third wave'. Not only does 'third wave' add to the suggestion of successive waves of feminism *overcoming* the previous one's mistakes, and thus buying into teleological predictions, it is also very strongly grounded in an American context. Nevertheless, I consider 'third wave' a necessary label for younger contemporary

European feminists to take on.

By labelling oneself 'third wave' one facilitates a situated reflection that is otherwise likely to be left aside. So-called third wavers are more or less, depending on their geographical location, used to having (institutionalised) feminism at their disposal. Feminism, in all its different guises (from state feminism to DIY), is something to be transferred; *it has already been there*, and as such it is something 'we' as a new generation can add to and change. It is not that this is only to be celebrated. Within the dominant narrative that Hemmings, but also, and in a slightly different form, Jackie Stacey,[11] has criticised, activist feminism is often considered to be found/founded in the 1970s, and to have disappeared in the 1980s with the move to the university. At least in many western European countries, and the U.S, younger feminists find themselves surrounded with institutionalised forms of feminism, yet at the same time are confronted with the norm of activism. My Swedish interviewees either apologised for not having 'started' as an activist or stressed the fact that in their opinion doing Women's or Gender Studies at universities today should be counted as a form of activism. By being explicit about transversalities in stories of third wavers, I want to argue that such a norm can possibly be changed. Now that the dominant narrative has been convincingly mapped out (Hemmings, Braidotti, Stacey), we have to ask ourselves: what does it do to (the reception of) Butler when her work serves as a generational marker? And what does it mean to actually *read* 1970s sources in the second Millennium, and work with conceptualisations of 'women' as having always been (at least possibly) multiple?

The round table discussion shows that my third wave statement is not uncontroversial. The round table consisted of at least two generations: a generation that has been working on the setting up of Women's Studies and a generation that has been employed by a university looking for Women's/Gender Studies experts. The fact that I found resistance within my generation and some recognition from without I would want to interpret as a welcome complexity. The statement, however, should become multi-axial, that is it should take into consideration more axes than just the generational one (think, in the context of the round table, about inter/disciplinarity, levels of institutionalisation, and national context).

Notes

[1] See Sonya Andermahr, Terry Lovell and Carol Wolkowitz (2000) *A Glossary of Feminist Theory*, Edward Arnold, New York: 86.

[2] Donna J. Haraway (1988) 'Situated Knowledges: The Science Question in Feminism and the Privilege of Partial Perspective' in *Feminist Studies* 14(3): 575-99.

[3] Sandra Harding (1986) *The Science Question in Feminism*, Open University Press, Milton Keynes.

[4] See for a *multi-layered* example: Adrienne Rich (1987) 'Notes Towards a Politics of Location' in Idem *Blood, Bread and Poetry*, Virago Press, London: 210-32.

[5] For my dissertation I conducted interviews and undertook participant observation at Tema Genus, the Interdisciplinary Gender Studies unit of Linköping University.

[6] Judith Butler (1999 [1990]) *Gender Trouble: Feminism and the Subversion of Identity* Routledge, London & New York.

[7] See Clare Hemmings (2005) 'Telling Feminist Stories' in *Feminist Theory* 6(2): 115-39 for a thorough analysis of this schema of, as Hemmings calls it, 'progress and loss.'

[8] Ibidem.

[9] Rosi Braidotti (2001) 'The Way We Were: Some Post-Structuralist Memoirs' in *Women's Studies International Forum* 23(6): 715-728, 718.

[10] Astrid Henry (2004) *Not My Mother's Sister: Generational Conflict and Third-Wave Feminism* Indiana University Press, Bloomington, Indiana.

[11] Jackie Stacey (1993) 'Feminist Theory: Capital F, Capital T' in Victoria Robinson & Diane Richardson (eds) *Introducing Women's Studies* Macmillan, London: 54-76.

Conclusion

Teaching Subjects: Journeying On

The collaboration within the *Travelling Concepts* group has been an adventure. It has been a journey in many ways, our own travelling between European cities being only one aspect. We also set out to develop ideas, to discuss concepts, starting with a broad range and by and by honing our focus and settling for 'Politics', 'Disciplines' and 'Generations' in relation to feminist pedagogy.

In a way, it seems that we did not manage to accomplish what we had intended. Some concepts seem to have been lost (still others were newly addressed). Within the conversation (first part of the booklet) we did not come to exchange ideas about the contents of feminist pedagogy in terms of its transformative or subversive potential and only marginally explored its forms, conditions and effects. We did not discuss teaching subjectivity as a concept in a more in-depth manner, but rather approached it via our own experiences and positions. In that way, we ended up focusing on the context and/or (pre)conditions of being teaching subjects – we were outflanking the teaching subjects, in a manner of speaking. However, what we witnessed simultaneously was how complex it is to interrogate teaching subjectivity from a multifaceted perspective as well as how differences of context and position as significant markers can block creative efforts towards fresh theoretical stands. And yet, the meaning of teaching subjectivity has been expanded by tracing some provocative ideas around generational status or disciplinary perspective, be it in subsequent discussions or comments to complement the original conversation in our papers (second part of the booklet), in which we developed insights into the practice and contents of feminist pedagogy and teaching Women's Studies.

With hindsight, it could be argued that what we have been doing is 'boundary work'. In the field of Science Studies, what Thomas Gieryn has coined 'boundary work' is being used for pointing to and unravelling the work that is done to create, negotiate and naturalise boundaries and dividing lines between fields of knowledge, both fields within the university and fields between the university and its surroundings.[1] Since boundaries are often naturalised, their social construction is often overlooked. Part One of the booklet shows the difficulties of laying bare all boundaries and the ways they intersect, because dividing lines cut across each other, and form a complex tapestry of forces. Part Two of the booklet tries to unravel differing instances of 'boundary work': what boundaries are created in European Women's/Gender Studies, and how can we make sense of them? What kinds of boundary work are done in this context, both in our favour and against us?

Each of us, obviously, pointed out her own most pressing concerns connected with teaching Women's/Gender Studies and/or Feminist Studies. These concerns are personal as well as political in a broader sense. They belong to the academic field as well as to that of (extramural) activism. Matters of the labour market were addressed, such as the marketability of Women's/Gender Studies along with its increasingly inextricable entanglement with gender mainstreaming. We brought up the issue of the importance of political context at the governmental level. Generational issues were taken up – what is it like to grow into being a teacher, how to negotiate classics (be it in the books or in the flesh) – and we address interrelations between one's own migrational experiences and one's teaching. All of these concerns boil down to the question of what it means for each of us to teach Women's/Gender Studies, in a very concrete manner. And so our initial meandering, orienting and situating ourselves has yielded fascinating insights into the practice of teaching Women's/Gender Studies and has maybe provided some answers to the question of who/what are teaching subjects – or, how to produce new thresholds for opening additional doors for scholars and students by both acknowledging and crossing differences and diversities. Thus, we find ourselves in line with Maria Puig de la Bellacasa's demand that we discuss openly the working conditions in the academy for (predominantly, but not only, young) scholars and teachers of Women's and Gender Studies.[2]

Although the journey may have brought us to a different destination than we had at first intended, our discussion could be considered as an example and a close-up view of the toils and joys of transnational collaboration in Women's/Gender Studies. The journey has not come to an end yet; the absence of a neat closure in traditional academic terms should not to be censored. On the contrary, it demonstrates how Women's Studies is represented by a fluid and multiple set of concepts that, while on the one hand rest on a sound theoretical and autonomous critical background, on the other are capable of raising questions and interrelating with other disciplines. Our collective efforts can also be seen as an incitement to others to reflect on their own situatedness and that of others, in order to better understand each other's stances, wishes, opportunities and dilemmas. At least we hope so.

Notes

[1] Thomas F Gieryn (1995) 'Boundaries of Science' in Sheila Jasanoff, et al. (eds) *Handbook of Science and Technology Studies*, Sage, Thousand Oaks: 393-443.

[2] Maria Puig de la Bellacasa (2002) 'Flexible Girls: A position paper on academic genderational politics' in: Luisa Passerini, Dawn Lyon, Liana Borghi (eds) *Gender studies in Europe/Studi di genere in Europa*, European University Institute, Robert Schuman Centre for Advanced Studies, San Domenico di Fiesole: 91-109.

Authors' Biographies

Josefina Bueno Alonso is Senior Lecturer in French Studies at Alicante University where she teaches French literature and is particularly interested in gender issues. Over the last few years, she has lectured on the literature and culture of French-speaking countries and her main focus of research is on francophone women writers, especially in the Maghreb. In her most recent publications she analyses postcolonial and gendered discourses in a francophone context.

Silvia Caporale Bizzini received her PhD at the University of Alicante (Spain) in 1994 and has been teaching and doing research at various universities in the UK, the USA and Canada. Since 1997 she has been Senior Lecturer at the University of Alicante where she teaches English Literature and Cultural Theory in the Department of English Studies. From 2002 to 2006 she has been the Director of the Women's Studies Centre at the University of Alicante and from 2003 to 2005 she was appointed Secretary of the Spanish University Association of Women's Studies. Silvia is currently working on the theory and representation of maternal autobiography as a (testimonial) political perception of the historically determined experience(s) of mothering.

Therese Garstenauer received her diploma in sociology and Russian language and literature at the University of Vienna in 2000. She has co-organised two Women's/Gender Studies conferences in Vienna. From 2004 to 2005, she has been a staff member of the Centre for Gender Studies at the University of Vienna and taught introductions to Gender Studies and Statistics. Presently, she is a staff member at the Department of Social and Economic History at the University of Vienna, writing her PhD thesis on research collaborations between Russian and 'Western' gender scholars, with a particular focus on how 'East' and 'West' are constructed in this context. For this thesis, she has done research in Russia, the UK and Germany.

Biljana Kašić is a feminist theorist, peace and civil activist and researcher from Zagreb, Croatia. She has a PhD in Political Sciences. In 1995, she co-founded the Centre for Women's Studies, Zagreb – the first centre of this kind in Croatia, and until 2006 she has been its coordinator. Besides her engagement at the Centre, she teaches at the Universities of Zadar and Rijeka (undergraduate programme) and the University of Zagreb (doctoral programme). She has been a guest lecturer at various universities worldwide. She recently created an email distance learning course 'Gender Perspective and the Balkans' for the Aleksanteri Institute, Helsinki, Finland. Related to her fields of interest (feminist epistemology, postcolonial theories, women's culture of resistance, theories of identity, and ethics) she has published and co-edited several books, studies and articles in Croatian and other languages.

Iris van der Tuin is a PhD student and junior teacher in Women's Studies at Utrecht University, the Netherlands. Her PhD project is on new feminist epistemologies and practices of European Women's Studies. Provisionally the dissertation is entitled 'Doing Gender'. Her publications include texts on Donna Haraway (her Companion Species Manifesto) and Karen Barad. As she is amongst the younger Dutch feminists who are spoken of as the next generation, she has also published on the state of the art of Dutch (academic) feminism. When it comes to her work as the coordinator of WeAVE – including the student forum of Athena – she has published in the Athena Volumes.

Websites of the respective Centres for Women's and Gender Studies

Centre for Women's Studies at the University of Alicante: http://www.ua.es/cem
Women's Studies at the University of Utrecht: http://www.genderstudies.nl
Centre for Gender Studies at the University of Vienna: http://www.univie.ac.at/gender
Centre for Women's Studies Zagreb: http://www.zenstud.hr

A note from Ann Kaloski of Raw Nerve Books

email: post@rawnervebooks.co.uk   web: www.rawnervebooks.co.uk

Dear Reader,

You have in your hands a book from Raw Nerve, a not-for-profit, micro publishing company that draws together people who work 'for love and politics' in order to further thinking about women's lives and feminism.

There was a lot of love and a lot of politics in this project! Travelling Concepts involved about thirty women and a few men living in many different countries – people who wrote, co-ordinated, edited, proofed, designed, organised printing and maintained the accounts. Working with varying styles of thinking and practices as well as sentence construction and referencing systems was an invigorating process from which, I think, we all benefited, and Raw Nerve has tried to retain the diversity of each group's product while bringing the books together into a harmonious series.

I'd like to express my gratitude to the adventurous Travelling Concepts women who wrote the four books – Silvia, Liana, Therese, Mina, Veronica, Dasa, Joan, Melita, Giovanna, Ulla, Enikő, Josefina, Päivi, Luz, Biljana, Soula, Iris, Eva, Sabine, Elena, Sara and not least Clare who facilitated the group so inspiringly and who was a hard-working co-editor. Thanks are also due to Liz, Lee and Karen; Dave and everyone at York Publishing Services; Bob; Ulla (again) and Josephine; the Centre for Women's Studies and Athena 2; and especially to our designer Hilary who has accommodated, interpreted and balanced the visions of a large group of sassy women with patience and care.

If you enjoyed this publication, consider buying one of the other books in the series (see the full list in the Series Preface). You are also invited to join in the wiki-based discussion at www.travellingconcepts.net

Ann